FROM THE ISLAND OF NEWFOUNDLAND

SALTWATER Mittens

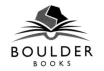

BOULDER
BOOKS

CHRISTINE LEGROW & SHIRLEY A. SCOTT

Library and Archives Canada Cataloguing in Publication

LeGrow, Christine, author
Saltwater mittens from the island of Newfoundland : more than 20 heritage knitting designs /
Christine LeGrow & Shirley A. Scott.

ISBN 978-1-77523-458-6 (hardcover)

1. Knitting--Canada--Newfoundland and Labrador--Patterns.
2. Mittens--Canada--Newfoundland and Labrador. 3. Knitting--Canada--
Newfoundland and Labrador--History. I. Scott, Shirley A., author
II. Title. III. Title: More than twenty heritage knitting designs.

TT819.C32N49 2018   746.43'20432   C2018-904385-7

© 2018 Christine LeGrow and Shirley A. Scott
Design and layout: Tanya Montini
Cover photo: Christine LeGrow
Editor: Stephanie Porter
Copy editor: Iona Bulgin
Printed in Canada

We acknowledge the financial support of the Government of Newfoundland and Labrador
through the Department of Tourism, Culture, Industry and Innovation.

We acknowledge the financial support for our publishing program by the Government
of Canada and the Department of Canadian Heritage through the Canada Book Fund.

Funded by the   Financé par le
   Government   gouvernement
   of Canada   du Canada   Canada

To those who brought it
To those who kept it
To those who hold it dear

CONTENTS

FOREWORD

To aficionados of traditional knits, this book from Christine LeGrow and Shirley Scott is a welcome addition to our libraries. Keen to explore the secrets of Newfoundland knitters, Christine and Shirley have collected and studied mittens from around the island, and they are now ready to share their findings with us.

Both are master technicians, with a passionate interest in unearthing and proclaiming patterns long practiced by knitters. Not surprisingly, this book describes the knitting techniques of Newfoundland knitters as sophisticated. Each stitch is placed just so to meet the requirements of a working man or a school-bound child—to avert the wind, to strengthen a stress point, to conserve warmth on the dampest days. Colours and other design elements bring delight to the wearer, avoid monotony for the knitter, and allow the knitting to reflect the environment in which it is created.

In the 1970s, when I joined the professional craft community, knitting was ubiquitous. Knitters proliferated at craft fairs; shops and festivals offered boundless choices. Today, despite the new enthusiasm for knitting across international networks, the traditional double-knit mittens of Newfoundland might very well be at risk of disappearing from our cultural lexicon. Knitters of traditional patterns, working endlessly to keep the hands of their families warm throughout the winter, are aging and diminishing in numbers. Already, patterns once widely practiced are disappearing and can only be found with determined searching by a knowledgeable eye. The patterns passed from generation to generation were not written down but depended on a community memory for their survival. Today, the mittens themselves must speak for the ingenuity and skill that went into each pair.

We are thankful that Shirley and Christine have taken on the search for these valuable artifacts and have built and interpreted the collection for us. They have the skill and interest to decipher patterns from the knitted objects and the insight to recognize their value and place in our heritage. Because of their work, double-knit mittens will not be found solely in museum holdings but will continue to clothe our winter days. Not only that, they have presented these patterns to us interwoven with stories of mittens, their knitters, and the tales that they tell. Sometimes nostalgic, often comical, these stories tell us as much about the personalities of Christine and Shirley as they do about knitting.

Saltwater Mittens from the Island of Newfoundland speaks to us of the joy and inspiration that knitting has brought to the lives of two spirited women. Page upon page, pattern upon pattern, this book will do the same for us.

Anne Manuel

Anne was Executive Director of the Craft Council of Newfoundland and Labrador from 1983 to 2016. She remains active in the professional craft community, and knits mittens when time allows.

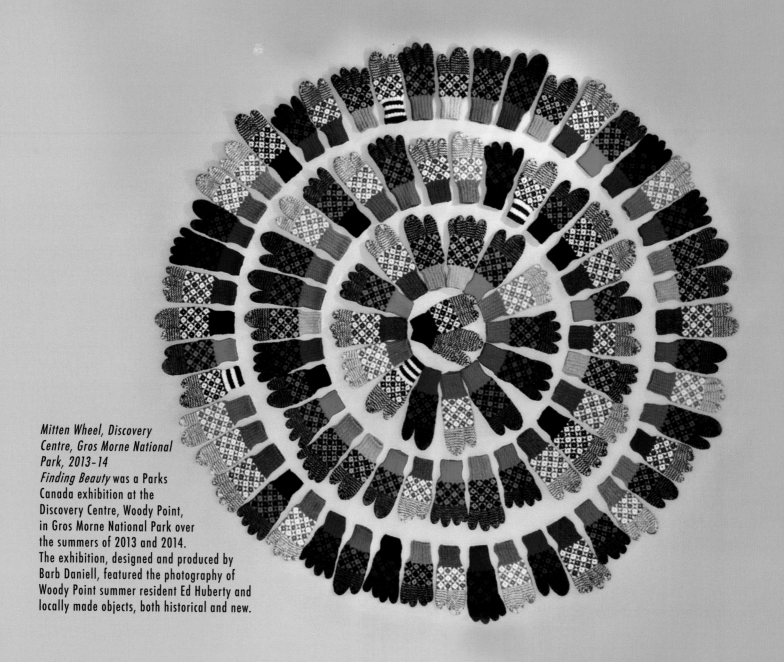

Mitten Wheel, Discovery Centre, Gros Morne National Park, 2013-14

Finding Beauty was a Parks Canada exhibition at the Discovery Centre, Woody Point, in Gros Morne National Park over the summers of 2013 and 2014. The exhibition, designed and produced by Barb Daniell, featured the photography of Woody Point summer resident Ed Huberty and locally made objects, both historical and new.

INTRODUCTION

On the island of Newfoundland, a tiny salt-scoured population who came to live here has clung to the edge of the continent like barnacles for hundreds of years. The hardship of early days can scarcely be imagined. How was anyone left alive? The land is beautiful but fierce. The sea is beautiful but treacherous. Never turn your back on it. So much bounty but so much loss. Light and dark. We see it reflected in our beloved knitting patterns.

Why do hard places produce great art? How does the struggle to survive wring beauty from rock, sea, and endless forest? It seems a mystery. Yet surely it does, for the Newfoundland mitten is truly an art form and an icon of our culture. One glance and we know its meaning. Home.

Good warm clothing has always been an essential barrier between us and extinction. Few people worked at desks in the old Newfoundland. Warm woollen mittens were the worker's friend, and the warmer the better. To hammer a nail, gut a fish, draw and haul water. To split birch for the stove. To hang clothes on a line. To shoot a seabird or snare a rabbit for the pot. Social life, too, required the finest mittens and gloves. For church, for ceremony, and for courting. For much of the year in our quirky climate of freeze, thaw, blow, and drizzle, good mittens made all tasks easier. This continues today. Our winter *ensembles* are serious business.

When he was goin' on the Labrador I'd have twelve, fifteen an' sixteen splittin' mitts for un.

—*DICTIONARY OF NEWFOUNDLAND ENGLISH*

For a long time only a few people in urban areas had the luxury of fine store-bought goods. For most Newfoundlanders all was supplied by the household. Much was made from yarn spun from fleece of the family sheep. The enormous task of

> **" I remember on one occasion I was attending a maternity case some miles from home ...We didn't feel right about going to bed when the patient was in such discomfort so out came the bag of wool.**
>
> **It was in the rough stage, meaning that it had merely been shorn from the sheep, washed, and teased out. The grandmother now carded with two wooden cards, these being wooden slabs with wire hooks covering one side of each, used to pull the rough wool into rolls. These were then passed to me and I would spin them into yarn with the spinning wheel. As soon as the yarn was ready, one of the younger girls commenced to knit mitts, and during that night of waiting a brand new pair was made for the young father.**
>
> **In between, I set to work cooking up a huge pot of stew ... "**

—MYRA BENNETT, *DON'T HAVE YOUR BABY IN THE DORY*

Old friends.
Photo: by permission of R. Abbott

clothing a large family must have been daunting and more than one pair of hands was surely needed for the work. Stories are told of how, before mass-produced synthetic clothing became generally available, some children in large families wore socks on their hands because mittens were in short supply. To be able to knit your own was such an advantage that young maids learned the skill at an early age.

Making a Newfoundland mitten requires specialized knowledge, as you are about to discover. Where did it come from? We can certainly rule out serendipity and other forms of casual discovery. Knitters must have recalled the fine work done in the Old Country and made it their gold standard in the New. With a hundred tasks at hand they took the time and trouble to pattern their mittens with intricate designs. We continue to marvel at this.

There have been many positive influences on Newfoundland knitters both past and present.

ANNA TEMPLETON (1916–95)

Miss T., as she was known, was a pioneer for craft training. She dedicated her life to it; she and her workers travelled to each rural area to share knowledge. Miss T. was the organizing secretary for the Jubilee Guilds of Newfoundland and Labrador and was instrumental in setting up formal craft vocational training in the province. The Anna Templeton Centre for Craft, Art and Design in St. John's is a witness to her legacy. You will find a great example of fine hand-knit trigger mitts in its display case of treasures.

NONIA, NEWFOUNDLAND OUTPORT NURSING AND INDUSTRIAL ASSOCIATION

Formed in 1920 to finance the work of nurses travelling and working in all outport areas, the association operated as a cottage industry. NONIA organized the best knitters on the island to knit high-quality items, including a variety of Newfoundland mittens. The goods were sold and the money helped pay nurses' salaries. While nursing is now under the aegis of government, the esteemed craft work of NONIA continues today, nearly a century later. Their retail premises on Water Street in St. John's is a landmark.

WOMEN'S INSTITUTE

This organization predated the Jubilee Guilds. The Newfoundland division was formed in 1929 and over the years worked predominantly with the women of the province. They sought to improve the quality of life for women and worked alongside others with similar goals. Almost 100 years later, they remain strong and still tied to craft. Their retail store on the Bonavista Peninsula stocks a fine selection of Newfoundland mittens.

OPERATION HOMESPUN

This knitting booklet of patterns was a project of Anna Templeton. Appearing under a number of titles, it was completed in 1980 and included patterns for all types of knitwear. It was the first opportunity many Newfoundland knitters had to see double-ball mitten patterns in print. Some well-known charts for use in mittens had names such as Spiderweb, Diamond, Hollow Squares, and Pyramid.

THE VOYAGE OF MICHAEL FLAHERTY'S MITTS

Strange things happen in Newfoundland, but none stranger than the voyage of Michael Flaherty's mitts.

Michael Flaherty is a talented ceramist whose work has been shown at prestigious galleries throughout the land. Michael owns a pair of very well-worn trigger mitts. They have been darned many times by numerous individuals but still had lots of wear left in them. Michael knows a thing of value when he sees it and he treasures his trigger mitts. His hands are very hardworking. So are his mitts.

Michael was working on a beach one day and had laid his mitts down. He was so engrossed in the task at hand that he didn't notice the tide coming in. When he reached for his mitts, they had bobbed out to sea on a wave.

A couple of days later he was working farther up the coast, much farther than any seagoing mitts should travel, when, there among the rocks and seaweed, he spotted his very own mitts. They had not drowned or drifted their separate ways (as some human couples do) but had washed ashore together. And to think it was Michael himself who found them—what were the chances?

Michael Flaherty's seagoing mitts.

Practicality was certainly one reason: a mitten double-knit with two colours is twice as warm and wind resistant as a mitten knit in a single colour. Pride in workmanship and the recognition of friends and neighbours may have been worth an equal amount to the maker. Newfoundlanders can often name the best knitters in their community. Making something well, even a humble mitten, earned prestige. This is true today.

We feel strongly that an unacknowledged artistic impulse was at work as well. It is the only way to account for the wonderful diversity of Newfoundland patterns. The importance of artistic sensibility in the domestic context is often overlooked.

Passing skills on is a critical element in continuity of tradition. Woman to woman, neighbour to neighbour, outport to outport, generation to generation, the ideal design for a good mitten stayed clear here. In later years literacy and communication improved survival chances for everyone and everything in Newfoundland. These same improvements might easily have imperilled traditional mitten knitting had not caring hands preserved it.

Formal as well as informal teaching has played a part in its survival. The province of Newfoundland and Labrador deserves praise for the quantity and excellence of its craft training initiatives over the years. From time to time our provincial government recognizes the significance of the craft sector in our economy. Authentic handcrafted items

Heirloom mittens.

I was late in life learning to knit. I was eight years old before I could knit.

—AMY BAILEY, IN *TRADITIONAL KNITTING IN NEWFOUNDLAND*, BY E.M. FITZPATRICK

AT THE AGE OF FIVE, AMY'S SISTER JULIE KNIT A PAIR OF MITTENS FOR HER FATHER, WITH EXCELLENT RESULTS. THIS SURELY MADE AMY REGARD HERSELF AS A SLACKER IN LIFE.

that speak of our heritage play a major role in branding this province for tourist promotion. Visitors seldom leave Newfoundland empty-handed, and mittens sell particularly well when tourists find themselves underdressed for our saucy weather. Craft products that depict the iconic status of mittens in Newfoundland culture are equally popular.

Regrettably, our cultural institutions sometimes see knitting as the poor sister because of its functionality. It may be looked on as simply "what Nan does." In museum collections, knitting has taken a back seat to quilting and rug hooking, for example. One reason for the lack of public recognition of knitting as a true folk art, here as elsewhere, is that mittens made for hard use were worn until they gave their last grasp. Sadly, no one could imagine donating them to a museum. This must change.

Popular gifts from Newfoundland.

While there are no public collections of vintage mittens in this province, there are many private collections. Every family has a pair or two of heirloom mittens safely put away, the last of their line. Newfoundlanders are ardent, passionate people who become so attached to their beloved mittens that they might almost be classed as intimate apparel. They symbolize care, safety, and love, and we can never overestimate the tremendous need for tokens of safety in a land where it is so often elusive.

The best way to preserve a tradition is to make sure people know what it is, why it is important, and how to do it. In *Saltwater Mittens from the Island of Newfoundland*, we present more than 20 intriguing designs that praise our heritage and proclaim our love of home. They are based on vintage mittens in our collection. We hope our work will help secure a strong future for these knitted cultural treasures.

Photo: P. Sobel

SOME TOASTY

Peter Sobol paints many beautiful pictures about Newfoundland life. His images of Newfoundland mittens are exceptional. Peter has rules about the mittens he paints. The person who knits them must be at least three score and ten years old and be able to tell a good story about why he should paint their mittens. For example, Joy (age 72) told Peter that he should paint her mittens because of her birth story. Her parents had seven children before her. When she was born, her parents felt joy because they hoped she was the final child to feed and raise. Peter painted her mittens.

Norway mittens.

ROOTS AND RELATIVES

In the world of hand knitting, Newfoundland mittens are special. Cultural traditions have stayed intact on this island. Isolation of every type haunted us in the past and it was certainly not seen as a benefit. But to the historian, the linguist, and the folklorist, isolation can be seen as a gift, and in this context Newfoundland's isolation was profound until the mid-20th century.

In some ways we were not at all isolated. From the days of earliest settlement there were civic, military, supply, kinship, and trade links with Britain and Europe. During the age of sail Newfoundlanders skimmed the waves of the seven seas. But the great wealth of Newfoundland did not trickle down much, the domestic economy remained small, and the material culture thin. The self-sufficient lifestyles of old continued. Lives depended on it.

The quickest, most cursory glance at a pair of Newfoundland mittens proclaims their origin. The striped wrist, the dark and light diamond or wave pattern, the salt and pepper top and palm, and the handy trigger finger shout out their birthplace. Travel to other parts of Atlantic Canada or New England and you may catch fleeting glimpses of near relatives of our mittens. The same striking two-coloured patterns and double construction has served us all well as part of a shared tradition.

◇◇◇◇◇◇◇◇◇◇◇◇◇◇◇◇◇◇◇◇◇◇◇◇◇◇◇◇◇◇◇

We all knew what a shepherd was, any fool did. A shepherd was a person who had nothing else to do but tend sheep unless he was a woman in which case he was a shepherdess. Shepherds were persons like Little Bo Peep and David who slew Goliath ...

—RAY GUY, "MYSTERIES OF THE WIDER WORLD"

◇◇◇◇◇◇◇◇◇◇◇◇◇◇◇◇◇◇◇◇◇◇◇◇◇◇◇◇◇◇◇

Voyage still farther on the North Atlantic—as far as Britain, Norway, the Faeroe Islands, and the Baltic countries—and you will reach the cradle of our mitten-knitting heritage. In each of these places we find stitch patterns like ours, and

Photo: P. Barry

NEWFOUNDLAND HERITAGE SHEEP

Sheep have been living in Newfoundland since the 16th century. Originally, European breeds were brought here by ship from the other side of the Atlantic. Living in the isolation of Newfoundland's rural communities, a distinctive breed developed. Once abundant, but now endangered, this hardy medium-sized sheep can live on whatever vegetation the landscape provides.

St. Jacques sheep are part of this breed. St. Jacques is a tiny coastal community in Fortune Bay on the south coast of Newfoundland. For most of its history, it was accessible only by coastal boats. There were no roads in or out until recent times. St. Jacques sheep have developed characteristics which enable them to survive harsh weather conditions and a very rough diet which includes the summer beach peas that grow there.

> **❝Why was a different matter. Ten or 12 sheep were plenty even for big families. Why would anybody keep so many sheep that it was one person's life's work to tend them?❞**
>
> —RAY GUY, "MYSTERIES OF THE WIDER WORLD"

versions of our salt and pepper pattern show up regularly too. Clearly, all ocean-going mittens share some DNA.

But there are differences, of course. European mittens were often knit in finer wool. Breeding sheep was a high art and very lucrative in Europe. Both hand and, after the Industrial Revolution, machine spinning were highly developed. Newfoundlanders made do with a spinning wheel and a handful of rugged sheep reared for survival, not for their soft wool.

How did knitting adapt to this hard country? We picture it this way: the Newfoundland knitter, generations after all ties with home had long disappeared, was left with a handful of diehard sheep and the memory of a few designs and techniques. It might all so easily have vanished. The sophisticated mittens of Europe might have been exchanged for something completely different and much simpler to make, but, instead, the old knowledge was passed from hand to hand through generations. Mittens became a little coarser but their essence was preserved. From these tenuous beginnings, like the settlement of Newfoundland itself, our knitting tradition flourished.

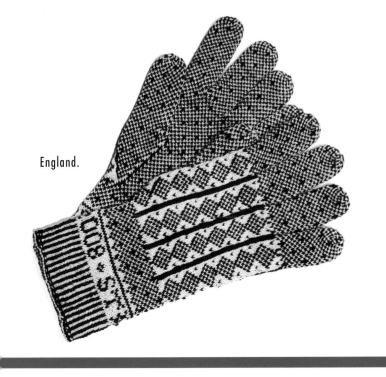

England.

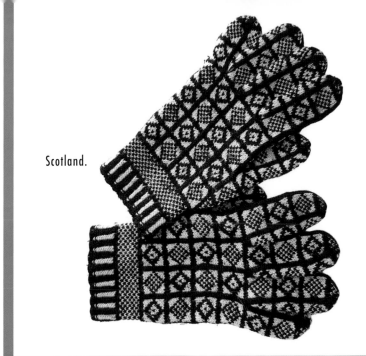

Scotland.

Estonia.

Nova Scotia.

The vintage collection.

THE VINTAGE COLLECTION

The patterns in this book are taken from three dozen vintage mittens collected in Newfoundland over a period of 40 years. They were acquired in various places on the island, beginning about 1980 when awareness of our precious and unique craft history was surfacing and when hand-knit mittens were still abundant and in general use. Mittens were easy to buy in those days. While many of these samples were bought at craft shops and craft shows, one pair was bought at a gas station and another at a restaurant. Several turned up in thrift shops. Yet another design was hastily charted from the treasured mittens of a friend's husband, who steadfastly refused to donate them to our archive but allowed us to quickly photograph them in the back seat of his car while he drove. One mitten was fished out of a puddle of slush, where it had been left to die a lonely death. That is how our curatorial adventure began.

Hand knits began to disappear from view here as in other places and inexpensive imported winter wear became ubiquitous. Traditional Newfoundland mittens, once worn everywhere, were on their way to becoming a tourist product rather than a time-tested form of practical work clothes. We feared they might disappear altogether in the headlong rush for prosperity and progress, for while it is true that hand knitting is indeed alive and well in Newfoundland, the great variety of patterns once seen in traditional mittens is no longer visible. In this book we have seized a welcome opportunity to document the creative diversity of traditional Newfoundland mittens and to add a few design flourishes of our own.

For every trip the boys made out fishing during a day they needed a pair of mitts, for the pair they wore previously would usually be wet and dirty from hauling the trap.

—MARY BARTLETT, IN "THE KNITTING OF TWO LADIES ON THE NORTHERN PENINSULA, GRIQUET AND ST. ANTHONY"

My dear, I knits awake, I knits asleep. I've done that several times—knit asleep. Best nap I've ever had ... I never knits on Sunday. I've done some worse things, but I never in my life knitted on Sunday ... I advises all young to knit.

—ELIZABETH WARNER, *KNITTING A GLOVE: ONE ASPECT OF ONE WOMAN'S KNITTING*

Preparing a book based on vintage mittens has been a technical adventure. Creating instructions by examining an actual mitten is like living inside another knitter's head for a period of time, anticipating the next stitch in her sequence, hesitating at her decision points, and stumbling where she perhaps stumbled in working out a tricky design. The task was often much more challenging than it looks. We admit that the ingenuity and complexity of some simple-looking patterns meant that, time after time, a pattern took a lot longer to write than it did to knit.

Based on our vintage collection, we can generalize only a little about the design of Newfoundland mittens, or "cuffs" as they are often called. We can safely say that their colours are most often subdued. This may date from the period when only undyed homegrown yarns were available or it may be simple common sense. Newfoundland mittens have always been working garments and some have done very hard work indeed, often covered in fish guts and worn to shreds. The fact that so much care was taken to create pleasing patterns in everyday clothing is a constant surprise, especially when so many pairs were needed for daily life and work.

"Trigger fingers" are characteristic of traditional mittens for men, although many mittens in our vintage collection do not have them. They were considered very practical and useful but they require an added element of attention and care in the making. Some think they are less warm than classic mittens. Fingers and thumbs in Newfoundland mittens are usually worked in the familiar and versatile "salt and pepper" combination. In this collection many designs feature now-popular trigger fingers for women.

The thumb gussets of days gone by also show ingenuity. A small number, possibly made from more recent printed patterns, favour the European style of construction, with no gusset whatsoever. Most gussets in the vintage collection, however, are worked in salt and pepper, outlined in either light or dark stitches. In double-ball (also called Fair Isle) knitting, this is actually the easiest way to insert a gusset that fits. Occasional examples of gussets with no outline stitch prove that it too was not a universal feature. We always include gussets in our designs because they improve fit.

Some vintage mittens had obvious flaws which we found endearing. In our instructions we occasionally make corrections and improvements that we hope the original knitter would thank us for.

Many old mittens show abundant signs of improvisation, not always with perfect success but always creating uniqueness. Some innovations are definite evidence of a stubborn artistic ambition on the part of the creator. Several knitters, for example, were determined to squeeze a large stitch count into a small size, surely one sign of bold ambition. We applaud their willingness to experiment and their pride in their work. Indeed the design sense of these home knitters of the past often prompts admiration. To take time from life's pressing demands to decorate a hard-working garment proves a love of beauty.

How closely did we stick to vintage designs when developing *Saltwater Mittens*? The majority of our stitch patterns were charted directly from them, often with considerable challenge. We have substituted a few modern construction techniques which we think are worthy improvements. Tidy jogless ribs, a two-round finger decrease, and the three-needle bind off are examples. These are our humble contributions to age-old techniques. A few patterns, such as Fogo Island Nine Patch, are original designs newly created in the traditional spirit.

Newfoundland patterns definitely do not have specific names entrenched in history and usage. We have assigned names indicating the provenance of the sample or according to our pleasure. This has been true fun.

GETTING STARTED

Newfoundland mittens require only the simplest equipment. This was especially important in days when supplies were scarce. Two balls of yarn of modest size, plus a few oddments for special designs, and a set or two of double-pointed needles puts you in business. Add two ring markers (or make some with loops of yarn) and a yarn needle to weave in the ends—and you're ready to go.

YARN

For most designs you need two contrasting shades of yarn, one dark and one light. The stronger the contrast, the bolder the look. Big Diamonds, Hangashore, and Mug-Up illustrate the power of just two colours. Using more than two colours is an option for some designs.

With the exception of striping in the wrist, most stitch patterns in traditional Newfoundland mittens use dark and light yarns in equal measure, a useful rule of thumb when estimating yarn quantities.

Saltwater mittens are made from the distinguished and venerable wool yarns from Briggs and Little Woolen Mills in Harvey Station, New Brunswick. We are devoted to its authenticity. It closely resembles the homespun yarn used in Newfoundland for centuries. The many interesting colours keep our spirits up as we work, and it is affordable. It is supremely hard working and hard wearing, a bonus in a place where many wearers still work outdoors and where the weather can be viciously unfriendly for long stretches. Newfoundland mittens and gloves are often created as fashion accessories today but they also qualify as serious outerwear.

Edith Thompson (1900–1966, Bonavista) was an avid knitter who referred to her straight needles as skivers and her double points as pins. Her pins, made of ivory or bone, were imported from England. Skivers were usually wooden; however, some were imported and made in the same materials as the pins. In later years, needles were sometimes made of Bakelite, but people continued to call them ivory.

We use three weights of Briggs and Little yarn.

Sport. 1-ply. 24 stitches = 10 centimetres on 3.00-millimetre needles. Put up 4-ounce skeins. 430 yards per skein. 40+ shades.

Regal. 2-ply. 20 stitches = 10 centimetres on 4.50-millimetre needles. Put up 4-ounce skeins. 272 yards per skein. 30+ shades.

Heritage. 2-ply. 17 stitches on 5.00-millimetre needles. Put up 4-ounce skeins. 215 yards per skein. 40+ shades.

Our instructions usually specify one skein of each colour. This is more than the amount actually needed. In many cases oddments of yarn are sufficient. Odd dye lots may sometimes be used as contrasting colours without detriment.

NEEDLES

Inexpensive double-pointed needles are all you need. In times past these were often homemade. Some of our friends learned to knit using 4-inch nails for needles. All of our instructions are written for circular knitting on double-pointed needles. As with other small circumference circular knitting projects, you may prefer the "two short circulars" method, or the magic loop method of knitting in the round. Both give excellent results. Instruction on both of these alternative techniques is available online.

The needle size suggested in the pattern should be viewed as a starting point only. In double-ball Fair Isle knitting great variations in gauge are found among knitters, particularly when they are first learning the technique. Tight knitters may need thicker needles and loose knitters thinner needles. Practice will develop a consistent gauge.

The three-needle bind off that gives such an attractive rounded top to the hand of a trigger mitt is easier if you have two thinner double-pointed needles handy. Size or length of these optional needles is unimportant as long as they are thinner than the needles used for the rest of the mitten.

This small outlay puts you in business, as it did the knitters of old.

SIZE

In days gone by, knitters were not unduly worried about the size of the finished product. In large families any garment was likely to fit some family member. Mittens were often knit large and loose because frequent cycles of hard use in salt water followed by drying behind a hot stove guaranteed some shrinkage. In this way, a custom fit was achieved. While this was possible with the homespun yarns made in those days, it is not guaranteed today.

We wrote each pattern for one specific size. As your expertise grows, you may find it possible to modify stitch patterns, but we do not recommend this for beginners. The complexity of the patterns and the need for symmetry in repeating sections and on front and palm means that

HANK

In Newfoundland this is not the name of a country singer from Nova Scotia, or of any man, for that matter. It is another name for skein of yarn before it is wound into a ball.

SIZE OF A TURNIP

An oddment of yarn, as described by a knitter. "I need a ball of medium grey wool to finish a sock, not a whole ball but a ball the size of a small turnip."

SKIVER, SKIVVER, OR SKYVER

1. Knitting needle
A skiver is a knitting needle with a knob on one end so that only the other end is free for knitting.

One of a set of two knitting needles; those making up a set of four will not be called skivers.

This term now often refers to any type of knitting needle.

2. A thin person; a small child.
—*DICTIONARY OF NEWFOUNDLAND ENGLISH*

A tale of
two gauges.

Alma Templeman (1921–2010, St. John's) loved to knit throughout her life and was very particular about the gauge and tension of a piece of knitted work. In her opinion, if something was knit too loose, she would tut-tut with a click of her tongue and exclaim, ❝ You could shoot gulls through that! ❞

altering stitch patterns is trickier than it seems. Instead, we suggest that changing needle size or yarn weight to produce a different gauge is the best way to modify the size of the finished product.

Although a bit experimental, this simple method can produce several sizes without changing a single number in any pattern. First, try using the suggested yarn with a larger needle. For many people this alone will make a ladies' pattern fit a man. For still larger sizes, change yarn as well as needles, perhaps using Heritage instead of Regal. You may also downsize mittens by first trying smaller needles, then perhaps a lighter weight of yarn as well.

In any pattern the hand, thumb, and fingers may be easily lengthened by adding rows of salt and pepper before shaping or topping off.

GAUGE

These mittens are tightly knit, which adds significantly to their warmth. A change in gauge will affect size and appearance, as described above.

FINISHING

Do not despair if your work looks lumpy and unpromising as you knit, especially if you are new to the technique. The touch of a steam iron will improve its appearance immensely. Do not press ribbing.

Men's trigger mitts.

Lukey's Boat
ST. JOHN'S NL

CHOOSE YOUR COLOURS

Mummers in Lukey's Boat.

Traditional Newfoundland mittens were knit with natural shades of homespun yarn because it was readily available. A fine range of browns, greys, and whites was always at the fingertips. Mittens knit with two highly contrasting shades of undyed yarn have a bold graphic appearance and a contemporary feel, even though the stitch patterns may be hundreds of years old. Great beauty is achieved with these colours, and many knitters continue to feel at home with this simple combination. Grey and white mittens continue to outsell all other colourways.

Why does this love of natural tones endure when the great wide world of colour awaits our needles today? One reason may be that the muted beauty of our dramatic landscape has such an impact from earliest years that earthy colours make us feel more at home. Our fickle weather, too, is so influenced by the ever-changing ocean that we are immersed in these quiet hues for much of the time. A quick look at the samples in this book shows that we delight in colours with the softness and subtlety of a Zen garden. The Spring Ice mitten illustrates this well. Perhaps Newfoundlanders feel happiest when their clothing blends with their surroundings.

Lukey's boat is painted green,
Ha, me boys!
Lukey's boat is painted green,
The prettiest boat that you've
ever seen,
A ha, me boys, a riddle-i-day!

—"LUKEY'S BOAT," TRADITIONAL

But like adventurous knitters everywhere, we also see our lovely island as a rich crayon box of colour. Crayon-box knitters are blissfully free of the practical need to match their mittens to their coats. Designs like the brilliant Fogo Island Nine Patch mitten came from the bright palette of our imaginations. Colourways such as these give a wonderful new look to traditional Newfoundland mittens and make them a desirable fashion accessory. Baccalieu, Fogo Island Nine Patch, St. Mary's Bay, and Signal Hill are particularly suitable for creating your own colour harmonies. And like a free-spirited Newfoundlander, you may choose to match your mitten to your house or boat.

Having knit with Briggs and Little yarns for many years, we have explored their colour options thoroughly, yet we continue to make exciting new pairings. There is much to be said for getting to know a single brand of yarn slowly and intimately.

Here are some colourways that we know and love. For our own amusement we have named them. Now you can add a touch of Newfoundland to your own brilliant creations. Exciting new discoveries await you. Why not start here?

BEST LOVED COLOURWAYS IN HERITAGE

Beet and Pea Salad. Mulberry. Fern.

Blueberry. Brown Heather. Mauve.

Camo. Khaki. Sheep's Grey.

Creamsicle. Orange. White.

Dogberry. Khaki. Orange.

Doppler Effect. Black. Bleached White.

Lemon Lime. Fern. Yellow.

Plum. Grape. Red Heather.

Safety First. Hunter Orange. Yellow.

Sunny Day. Light Blue. Yellow.

Watermelon. Fern. Pink.

BEST LOVED COLOURWAYS IN SPORT

As seen in multicolour Fogo Island Nine Patch mittens.

Berry Jam. Mulberry. Mauve. Orange. Red Heather. Green Heather. Light Green. Rust.

The Eighties. Blue Heather. Red. Pink. Dark Green. Light Green. Light Blue. Navy.

Funky. Scarlet. Violet. Royal. Orange. Rust. Paddy Green. White.

Photo: L. LeGrow

Fogo Island Nine Patch.

Nan's Quilt. Peacock. Washed White. Paddy Green. Scarlet. Pink. Violet. Fern Green.

BEST LOVED COLOURWAYS IN REGAL

Barrenlands. Dark Grey. Lilac. Forest Brown. Red BWO.

Camo. Dark Brown. Fir Green. Light Brown.

Cape Bonavista. Red. Bleached White.

Coconut Candy. Briar Rose. Washed White.

First Light. Midnight Blue. Horizon Blue.

Gannet. Washed White. Grey. Yellow WO. Midnight Blue.

Hot Buttered Rum. Forest Brown. Yellow WO.

Lukey's Boat. Dark Green. Bleached White.

Dusty Republic. Briar Rose. Natural White. Sage.

Republic. Briar Rose. Bleached White. Dark Green.

Row House: Summer. Scarlet. Yellow WO. Meadow Green. Royal Blue.

Row House: Autumn. Red. Forest Brown. Plum. Sage.

Row House: Winter. Light Maroon. Forest Brown. Navy. Fir Green.

Salvage Sunset. Dark Grey. Copper. Blue BW. Royal Blue.

St. Mary's. Dark Green. Fundy Fog. Quoddy Blue. Yellow WO.

Valentine. Red. Briar Rose.

Mug-Up in Dogberry.

Baccalieu in Dusty Republic.

Mug-Up in Sunny Day.

Mug-Up in Watermelon.

Baccalieu in Barrenlands.

St. Mary's Bay in Gannet.

Republic trio.

Mug-Up long trigger mitts.

NEWFOUNDLAND MITTENS EXPLAINED
from Cast On to Cast Off

What exactly is a Newfoundland mitten?

Judging from historical sources such as the *Dictionary of Newfoundland English*, nearly any hand covering qualifies, regardless of the number of fingers on it. A splitter's mitt might have none, a Torbay mitt one. A pair of five-fingered mittens would have an entire handful.

Because it originated as folk knitting without the benefit of written instructions, the terminology of Newfoundland knitting has been fluid. Newfoundland knitspeak is always highly descriptive. Some knitters referred to mittens as "thumbies." A splitter's mitt, worn when gutting fish, was called a "cut throat." A header's mitt was sometimes called a "gulbin," a term of no known derivation. In *Saltwater Mittens*, we have reluctantly adopted more consistent if less entertaining terminology.

Here is how a Newfoundland mitten is made.

CAST ON FOR THE WRIST

All of our patterns begin with casting on for the wrist and are knit from the bottom up. Mainlanders often call this part of the mitten "the cuff," but in Newfoundland a pair of mittens is commonly referred to as a "pair of cuffs," so we use the term "wrist" to avoid confusion.

Top-down mittens are sometimes knit in Newfoundland, but we prefer the more usual way of beginning at the wrist. No special cast-on method is required. We most often begin with the darker colour for symmetry.

WHICH RIB?

The wrist is always ribbed to ensure a snug fit. Every sort of rib has been used over the years, with knitters having their favourite styles. Single rib and twisted rib are common. We

Customer: **Do you have any five-finger mittens?**
Knitter: **You mean gloves?**
Customer: **No not those, the five-finger mittens! The Newfoundland ones! You know. They are salt and pepper with patterns, and the thumb and finger and the other three fingers!**

THUMBY

Heavy fingerless mitten.

MITT

Knitted woollen glove with separate sheaths for thumb and forefinger or for thumb alone; Cuff…. They have another one with three fingers—a palm there was would take three fingers an' a thumb. That'd be the mitt.

TORBAY MITT

Torbay mitts were hand-knit from wool of local sheep, carded and spun by hand. They were usually black and white standard pattern, some with thumb and one finger, some with just the thumb.

SPLITTER'S MITT

On his left hand the splitter wears a "splittin'cuff," a kind of fingerless wool mitten.

SPLITTING

One of the first items a girl would be expected to knit (after learning "garter stitch," i.e. plain knitting, on a head band or garters) was a pair of long stockings for herself, or, she might do a "splitting mitt" for her father.

CUFF

A thick, usually fingerless mitten, made of wool, swanskin or leather, worn in winter.

Mittens to wear upon the hands. They resemble those made use of by hedgers in England.

A fisherman's heavy mitten, often with the fingers cut off, used to protect the hand in hauling lines or splitting fish.

To lick one's cuff: to submit to any humiliation in order to secure an object.

—DICTIONARY OF NEWFOUNDLAND ENGLISH

… There was boiled duff, cold duff, and sugar boiled in knitted cuffs …

—"THE KELLIGREWS SOIREE," JOHNNY BURKE

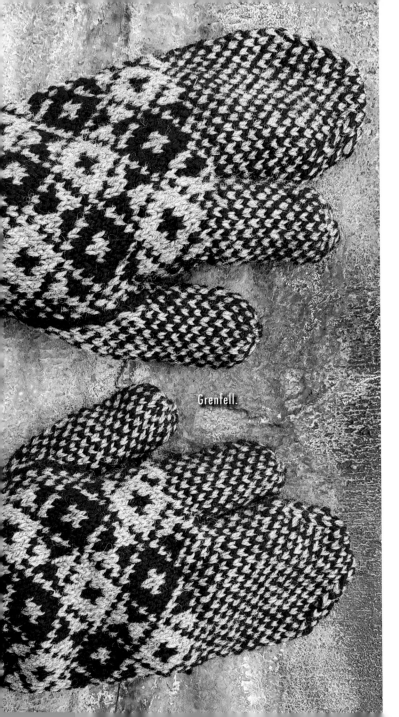

Grenfell.

choose (knit 2, purl 1) rib most often. It is firm but stretchy and showcases the colours of the yarn. Feel free to use any rib that you like.

HOW LONG?

The optimum length for an adult seems to be 24–27 rounds. You may use any number of rounds but, as a general rule, the longer the ribbed wrist, the better the fit. A skimpy mitten is an unloved mitten no matter how beautiful.

Our Mug-Up Trigger Mitt, with its long, elegant wrist, is a wonderful example of a new twist for traditional mittens. This design banishes cold air from your sleeve forever and in such a fashionable way. The tapering is achieved by changing the needle size.

STRIPE SEQUENCES

The wrists of mittens are usually striped. Newfoundland knitters have often used horizontal stripes to add a touch of colour to knitted work the easy way. When developing new designs, we look forward to dreaming up new stripe sequences for the wrist.

The most common form of striping over the years is one round of dark followed by one round of light. It continues to please. Working with more than two colours, as in Fogo Island Nine Patch, creates a wonderful look. Our Nor'easter mittens have a "storm surge" stripe sequence. Mittens with three broad stripes have a bold graphic appearance and are the best way to learn to make tidy jogless stripes. Tidy jogless stripes are an innovation not seen in vintage mittens.

Tidy stripes eliminate the colour bleed that occurs in purl stitches on the first round of a new colour. A tidy stripe must be at least two rounds deep. See "Abbreviations, Tips, and Techniques for Double-Ball Knitting."

Jogless stripes make the first round of a new colour blend seamlessly with the old colour without the steps and stairs caused by changing colours. It may be worked on stripes of any number of rounds.

Tidy jogless stripes must be broad, because too many tidy stripes will flatten the wrist significantly.

The Baccalieu mitten has detailed instructions for making these entirely optional modern wonders that neaten your work. You may use them in any of our designs.

Photo: J. Laaning

Nor'easter.

THUMB GUSSET

Our mittens have functional thumb gussets which guarantee freedom of movement and a good fit. This sets them apart from their European relatives that often have no gusset at all or merely a rudimentary one.

Newfoundland thumb gussets are usually outlined boldly in a solid colour, with the gusset stitches made in alternating salt and pepper sandwiched between the outlines. Gusset outlines may have begun life as a simple way to make the numbers work, for Newfoundland mittens are indeed numerically demanding. Outlines may be dark or light. This collection has both.

INCREASING FOR THE HAND

Increases blend in well when they are made into knit stitches, but this is a matter of choice.

Any increase method will do the job, but knitting into the front and back of the stitch tends to be visible and we like it least. We prefer a lifted increase worked into a knit stitch of the rib. It transitions nicely into the pattern on the hand.

Increases may be made in a knit round inserted after the last round of ribbing or inserted into the rib itself. Plan your stripes accordingly.

The increase round should be dark, if dark is your main colour, to minimize visibility.

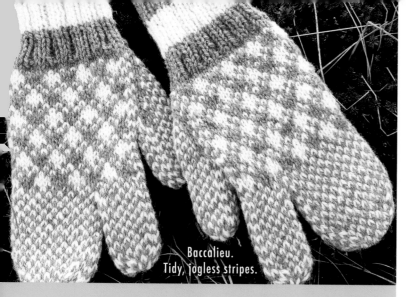

Baccalieu.
Tidy, jogless stripes.

I first remember when I was two years old of sending [a] mitt to Mr. Smith, who years after was Lord Strathcona, to get candies as my father was going up to Northwest River hauling a sled, for we had no dogs and the snow was hard. Perhaps he would be away for a week. We lived a long way from anyone. I don't remember when he came home, a while after dark. I was very tired and was asleep when he come. I jumped up; I thought of my mitt. My father took me on his knee and gave me the mitt full of candies. It was sewn up with twine. Mr. Smith had sewn it up. I gave some all around, for I thought I had so much candies.

—MARGARET BAIKIE, *LABRADOR MEMORIES: REFLECTIONS AT MULLIGAN*

THE HAND

Here the fun begins! Patterns on traditional Newfoundland mittens dazzle the eye and are a joy to knit.

Diamonds are undoubtedly the most popular pattern. Older knitters speak of "diamonds, quarter diamonds and half diamonds." They may be vertical, horizontal, or both. Some mittens contain more than one type. Completely symmetrical, tessellated diamond designs are among the easiest patterns to knit from memory. Little triangles build into big diamonds stitch by stitch. Single diamonds acquire many facets as coloured round builds on coloured round. Multiple diamonds are often hidden in one design. Grenfell and Mummers mittens are good examples of this.

In Newfoundland, diamond patterns are also used as architectural embellishments on houses, sheds, fishing rooms, and other waterfront buildings. A diamond window is an easy way to add charm and individuality to a home. Since the simplest diamonds are simply squares turned sideways, they did not need to cut a special piece of glass, a benefit in the days when materials were scarce and costly.

Is our love of diamond patterns purely practical? Possibly not. We have heard them referred to both as "God's eyes" and "devil's eyes," suggesting a significance buried in folk belief. Our Big Diamonds mitten pays homage to the diamond windows of some of our best loved buildings.

Wave patterns are second in popularity to diamond

patterns. Nor'easter and Blowin' a Gale are fine examples of wave mittens.

The palms of Newfoundland mittens are always knit in salt and pepper. It is the warmest stitch pattern of all. Patterns on the front of the mitten have a fixed number of stitches to ensure symmetry. Alter them at your peril. But adding and subtracting a few stitches is easily done in salt and pepper on the palm, a quick and easy way of customizing fit. The extensive use of this warm stitch is a touch of practical Newfoundland genius.

The pattern on the hand most often has the same number of rounds as stitches. This patterned section is followed by a number of rounds of continuous salt and pepper on the upper part of the hand to achieve the required length. The mitten may be lengthened by adding a few more rounds at this point.

SHAPING THE TOP

When a mitten reaches the tip of the little finger, it is time to shape the top. The top is subtly sloped by working paired decreases at four points in the round, positioned as on the toe of a sock.

When knitting a classic mitten with no trigger finger, there is a choice of top shapings. The picket-fence top, seen in Signal Hill mittens, for example, comes to a point at the top of the mitten. Decreases are made on every round to create a picket-fence top. It fits very well.

To make a rounded top, as seen on the Mummers mitten, two decrease rounds are followed by one round without decreases.

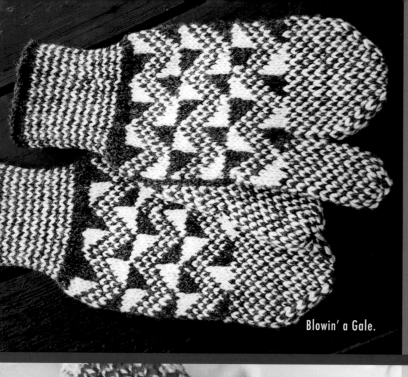

Blowin' a Gale.

Signal Hill. Picket fence.

Mummers. Round top.

Spring Ice. Patterned forefinger.

This creates a gentle slope. When the correct length is reached, the rounded top is finished by a three-needle bind off. Not seen on vintage mittens, it is a signature *Saltwater Mittens* technique that involves turning the mitten inside out and knitting the top together. This finishing touch is impeccable. See "Abbreviations, Tips, and Techniques for Double-Ball Knitting."

Trigger mitts always have rounded top shaping on the hand portion because there are too few stitches for a picket fence.

Mitten designs such as Blowin' a Gale modify the top shaping to suit the design.

CASTING OFF

Casting off is sometimes known as "topping off." Classic mittens with a picket-fence top need no cast off. The tail of yarn is threaded through the few remaining loops and then secured. Round tops are finished with the innovative three-needle bind off. In days gone by, round tops may have been grafted.

THUMB AND TRIGGER FINGER

One school of thought about primate evolution suggests that an opposable thumb and finger is the decisive development that set *homo sapiens* on the road to world domination. Clever Newfoundland knitters figured this out long ago and made sure that mittens did not hinder the development of civilization.

"Trigger finger" is actually a term of art today. These mittens are used for much more than hunting. Outdoor work is impossible without the trigger finger. It makes a thousand common tasks much easier. Even townie lifestyles demand trigger fingers. How else to eat lunchtime chips from the chip truck? Adjust your sunshades? One knitter of days gone by referred to the trigger finger as "the claw."

Patterned trigger fingers are a fashionable innovation.

Some people believe that trigger fingers are only for men. Nonsense! Today they are a gender-neutral fine fashion statement. We have included many patterns for ladies' trigger finger mitts in this collection.

Gloves are an exercise in neatness for the maker and a great way to practice finger construction. Try our Nor'easter pattern to sharpen your skills. Picking up stitches in salt and pepper pattern certainly is not child's play.

Baccalieu classic mitten.

DEGREES OF DIFFICULTY

We would love to tell you that Newfoundland mittens are simple to knit, but it's just not true. In the great world of folk knitting, they are a surprisingly sophisticated product. We are continually astonished by the complexity of the mittens in our vintage collection and have identified several points in the construction process where specialized knowledge is required. Busy women with large families and huge responsibilities had this knowledge and shared it. We pay homage to them.

If you enjoy knitting small items for children, we suggest that you begin your Newfoundland mitten journey with Wee Ones Thumbless Mitts for Babies. It provides experience in the essential techniques of carrying colours and shaping in salt and pepper pattern without the complexity of adding a thumb gusset or thumb. With several stitch patterns to choose from, you may want to linger here for a while. Then move to Little Corner Boy Mittens for Youngsters. They contain all the elements of an adult mitten but are much faster to complete.

Begin your adult mitten knitting voyage with the Baccalieu Mitten. We teach this design in our workshops because it features one of the best known and easiest of stitch patterns. There are no more than three adjacent stitches of a single colour in any row, a great advantage for beginners, yet an endless variety of colour combinations is possible. The Baccalieu pattern is a satisfying mitten to knit, and features

Who Knit You?

This expression is perhaps best described by folklorist Jasmine Paul, one of a new generation of professionally trained Newfoundland knitters. She named her line of hand-knitwear Who Knit You? This question fondly asks, "Where did you come from? Who are your parents? Who knit ya?"

Photo: J. Loaning

Mummers classic mitts.

options for trigger mitts, classic mittens with a picket-fence top shaping, and simple fingerless wristers. If you make all three, you'll know all the secrets of old and can take your place among the Newfoundland knitters of years gone by. The Mummers Classic Mitt is also one of the easier patterns for those just learning the ropes of double-ball knitting. It is a very old design.

We have labelled each Saltwater Mitten design by level of difficulty. Since we cannot supervise in person, we also offer a few motivational encouragements, in the manner of fortune cookies.

EASY DOES IT ✳

Not simple but a good place to start. Work slowly and carefully to succeed. Remember to breathe.

TANGLY ✳✳

The word speaks for itself. Keep your wits about you and success will be yours. You'll earn your stripes with this design. Remember to breathe.

OVER THE WHARF ✳✳✳

Worse things happen at sea! Persevere with this challenging experience and you'll make a work of art. As you progress, think of those who have knit before you. Mighty oaks from little acorns grow. Remember to breathe.

Little Corner Boy.

Nor'easter.

ABBREVIATIONS, TIPS, AND TECHNIQUES FOR DOUBLE-BALL KNITTING

CARRYING YARNS

Always carry the dark yarn on the left and the light yarn on the right to prevent streaks in the colour work. This is essential in double-ball knitting.

DOUBLE-POINTED NEEDLES

Straight needles with points at both ends, usually used in small circumference circular knitting. Our instructions are written for sets of four needles, three to hold the stitches and one working needle.

JOGLESS STRIPES

These have no "stair step" at the point where a new colour is joined at the beginning of a round. Use them on the wrists of mittens for a professional touch. To make stripes jogless, work the first round of the new colour in the required stitch. On the second round of the new colour, slip the first stitch of the round to the right needle purlwise without working it, then continue knitting to the end of the round. This shifts the beginning of the round one stitch to the left. When wrist ribbing is complete, reinstating the original beginning of the round is optional. Jogless stripes are often combined with tidy stripes.

MAKE 1 LEFT (M1L). MAKE 1 RIGHT (M1R).

These paired increases are used in the thumb gusset of a Newfoundland mitten and are made with the colour indicated on the gusset chart. The backward loop (half hitch) method of increasing is most appropriate for these projects. Other methods may also be used.

PICKET-FENCE TOP SHAPING

A picket-fence shaping comes to a point at the top of a mitten. To create a picket-fence top, work decreases in salt and pepper on every round until too few stitches remain to work a full repeat. Break yarns, thread one yarn through the remaining loops, draw tight and secure. See also Round Top Shaping.

ROUND TOP SHAPING

To create a round top, two salt and pepper decrease rounds are followed by a round with no decreases, ending shaping with a no-decrease round. Trigger mitts usually have a round top. Classic mittens may have either.

S&P. SALT AND PEPPER PATTERN

This distinctive stranded colourwork pattern is a mainstay in Newfoundland knitting, filling areas such as thumbs, trigger fingers, palms of hands, mitten tops, and other areas requiring shaping. This famous stitch is warm and versatile. It gives Newfoundland mittens their character. When worked on an odd number of stitches, it has a seamless appearance and the beginning of a new round is invisible. Mittens, thumbs, or individual fingers may be lengthened by adding rounds of S&P as needed before shaping. It is a two-round pattern.

Salt and Pepper Pattern (S&P) is worked on an odd number of stitches. **Round 1.** (K1 with Dark [K1D], K1 with Light [K1L]), repeat to end of round, ending with D. **Round 2.** (K1L, K1D), repeat to end of round, ending with L.

Decreasing in S&P at the top of a mitten requires special care. On odd numbered rounds, decreasing will create 2 adjacent stitches of the same colour. On the following even numbered decrease round, these stitches will be worked together, restoring the correct colour sequence. On Newfoundland mittens, the decreases are positioned in 4 points.

Decrease Round 1. Front. K1 with correct S&P colour, SSK with next colour in the sequence, work S&P until 3 stitches remain on front needle, K2tog with the same colour as the stitch just made, K1 in correct colour of S&P. **Palm.** Work as for front (4 stitches decreased).

Decrease Round 2. Front. K1 in S&P, SSK with next colour in the sequence, S&P to last 3 stitches of front, K2tog with next colour in the sequence, K1 in S&P. **Palm.** Work as for front (4 stitches decreased).

SSK. SLIP, SLIP, KNIT

A left-leaning decrease used to shape knitted pieces. It has a neater appearance than SKP (slip 1, knit 1, pass slipped stitch over), which does the same job. Slip two stitches knitwise one at a time. Insert left needle through the front of these two stitches from left to right and knit them together with required colour through the back of the loop. SSK is one of two decreases used to shape the top of mittens. The other decrease is K2tog, which leans to the right.

THUMB AND FINGER DECREASES

Thumb, trigger finger, and glove fingertips require two decrease rounds in S&P to complete.

Finger Decrease Round 1. (K1 with correct colour in the S&P sequence. K2tog with next colour in the sequence. K1 in S&P). Repeat to end of round, working any leftover stitches in S&P. Adjacent stitches in the same colour will be eliminated in the next round. **Finger Decrease Round 2.** (K1 with correct S&P colour. K2tog with next colour in the S&P sequence). Work any leftover stitches in S&P. Break yarns. Thread through remaining stitches and secure.

Substituting SSK for K2tog is valid, but it causes the work to spiral in the opposite direction.

THUMB GUSSET INCREASES

Thumb gussets are an important feature of Newfoundland mittens. Gusset increases are made inside an outline stitch and may be dark or light, as the chart indicates. Any good increase method will work, but we prefer the backward loop method and teach it in all our workshops. It is formally known as the half hitch cast on or half hitch increase.

Professional-looking gusset increases also lean to the right and left as indicated on the chart. Use M1R and M1L increases for the neatest work.

TIDY STRIPES

Tidy stripes are not traditional, but they have a handsome finished appearance. We have coined the name but the technique is an old one. They are used in the wrist ribbing of mittens. The colour of one tidy stripe does not bleed into the colour of an adjacent stripe. A tidy stripe must be at least two rows deep. To make stripes in ribbing tidy, work the first round of each new colour in plain knitting. Resume ribbing on the second round of the new colour. Tidy stripes may be combined with jogless stripes.

THREE-NEEDLE BIND OFF

This is a signature technique in *Saltwater Mittens*. It is used to finish a round-top mitten smoothly and is worked on the wrong side with the mitten turned inside out. It is used in place of two-colour grafting, a much more difficult technique.

Place the stitches of the front on a piece of waste yarn. Place the stitches of the palm on another piece of yarn. Turn mitten inside out to bind off. Return stitches to 2 double-pointed needles. To make joining easier, use needles that are thinner than those used on the garment. This is optional. Hold these needles parallel to one another. The needle with the greater number of stitches must be facing you.

K1 with the long tail of D and a third thin double-pointed needle. This puts 1 stitch on the working needle. Then knit together 1 stitch from the front-holding needle with one stitch of the opposite colour from the rear-holding needle. Two stitches are now on the working needle. Pass first stitch on working needle over second stitch to cast it off. One stitch remains on the working needle. Continue to knit together 2 stitches of opposite colour from the holding needles and slipping the first stitch over second stitch on the working needle until 1 stitch remains on the holding needle. Fasten off and darn ends. Turn mitten right side out.

BACCALIEU
Classic Mittens, Trigger Mitts, or Wristers for Ladies

DEGREE OF DIFFICULTY: * EASY DOES IT

Baccalieu Island (N48°07'49", W52°48'05") stands sentinel at the mouth of Conception Bay, an area of exceptional marine richness. The name, which comes from the Spanish/Basque/Portuguese word for codfish, has been in use for 500 years. Now an uninhabited island, Baccalieu remains a navigational watchword. The Baccalieu Island Ecological Reserve is an important seabird refuge.

Baccalieu is a great way to begin your mitten-knitting voyage to Newfoundland. The tidy jogless stripes on the wrist are a refinement well worth mastering.

SIZE

Ladies' Medium. Circumference: 8 inches (20 cm). Length from cast on to tip: 11 inches (28 cm). Length is adjustable. Change gauge to change size.

MATERIALS

1 skein Briggs and Little Regal 2-ply worsted weight wool in Dark (D). 1 or more skeins of Regal in Light (L). If using more than 1 Light colour, oddments are sufficient. 1 set of 4.00 mm double-pointed needles. Ring markers.

GAUGE

22 stitches x 24 rows = 4 inches (20 cm).

*We were bound home in October
from the shores of Labrador
Tryin' to head a strong nor'easter
and snow too,
But the winds swept down upon us
makin' day as dark as night
Just before we made the land
off Baccalieu.*

—"THE CLIFFS OF BACCALIEU," JACK WITHERS

BACCALIEU CHART (6 stitches x 8 rows)

6	5	4	3	2	1	
	●		●		●	8
●	●	●				7
●	●	●				6
	●		●		●	5
●		●		●		4
			●	●	●	3
			●	●	●	2
●		●		●		1

THUMB GUSSET CHART

●		●		●		●		●		●		●	14
●	←		●		●		●		●	→	●	13
●		●		●		●		●		●	12
●		⇦	●		●		●	⇨		●	11
●			●		●		●			●	10
●			←		●		→			●	9
●				●		●				●	8
●				⇦	●	⇨				●	7
●					●					●	6
●				←	●	→				●	5
●				●		●				●	4
●				⇦	●	⇨				●	3
●					●					●	2
←					●					→	1

● K1D   Empty square = K1L

→ Make 1 Right with D   ← Make 1 Left with D

⇦ Make 1 Left with L   ⇨ Make 1 Right with L

SALT AND PEPPER PATTERN (S&P)

Worked over an odd number of stitches.

Round 1. (K1D, K1L). Repeat to end of round.

Round 2. (K1L, K1D). Repeat to end of round.

Work charts from right to left and bottom to top. Keep D always on the left and L always on the right to prevent streaks in colour work. Introduce a new contrasting L colour on Rounds 5–8, if desired, and throughout the top, as pictured. Work the wrist in a striped pattern of your choice or as below. Instructions are for both hands unless otherwise stated. Instructions for the classic mitten, trigger mitt, and wrister are the same to the end of pattern Round 24.

Wrist. Tidy Jogless Stripes. With D or the colour of your choice, cast on 36 stitches and join in a round, being careful not to twist. Work 8 rounds in (K2, P1) ribbing. Break yarn.

Next Round. Tidy Stripe. Join L and knit this round *with no purl stitches* to create a tidy stripe.

Next Round. Jogless Stripe. Slip the first stitch of the new colour purlwise to the last needle without working it, thereby shifting the beginning of the Round 1 stitch to the left. K1, P1, (K2, P1) to last stitch, K1. Rib 7 more rounds as set. Break yarn.

Next Stripe. Join D and repeat 1 round of tidy stripe and 1 round of jogless stripe, resuming ribbing with P1. Work 7 rounds more ribbing in this colour.

Increase for Hand. With D, knit 1 round, increasing 11 stitches evenly spaced (47 stitches).

Place 24 stitches on the front needle. Divide the remaining stitches conveniently on 2 needles for palm. The front will be worked in Baccalieu pattern and the palm in salt and pepper.

Round 1. Front. Work Round 1 of Baccalieu chart 4 times on front stitches. **Palm. Right Hand.** K1D, K1L. Place marker. M1R with D, to create the right-leaning gusset outline stitch. K1D to establish the point of the thumb gusset. M1L with D to create the left-leaning gusset outline stitch. Place marker. There will be 3 adjacent D stitches. Beginning with K1L, work in S&P to end of round. **Left Hand.** (K1D, K1L) 10 times. Place marker. M1R with D to create the right-leaning outline stitch. K1D to establish the point of the thumb gusset. M1L with D to create the left-leaning outline stitch. Place marker (there will be 3 D stitches together). Work in S&P to end of round.

You have set up the Baccalieu stitch pattern on the front, created the point of the thumb gusset on the palm, inserted 2 D outline stitches on either side of the gusset stitch, and set up the S&P on the palm.

Round 2. Work Round 2 of Baccalieu 4 times on the front. Work the palm in S&P to marker. Slip marker. Work Round 2 of the thumb gusset chart between the markers as follows: K1D outline stitch. K1L gusset stitch. K1D outline stitch. Slip marker. Work in S&P to end of round.

Round 3. Work Round 3 of Baccalieu 4 times on the front. Work the palm in S&P to marker. Slip marker. Work Round 3 (increase round) of thumb gusset chart to next marker. Slip marker. S&P to end of round.

Continue working successive rounds of Baccalieu on the front of the mitten, the thumb gusset chart inside the markers, and the rest of the palm in S&P, until the thumb gusset chart has been completed. There are now 15 gusset stitches inside the markers.

Next Round. Work Baccalieu pattern on the front. Work S&P on the palm to marker. Remove marker. Put next 15 thumb gusset stitches on a holder. Remove marker. Cast on 1 stitch in the correct colour to bridge the gap. Work S&P to end of round. Thumb gusset is now complete. **Next Round.** Work Baccalieu pattern on the front. Work S&P on the palm.

Hand. Repeat the last round until 24 rounds of Baccalieu pattern are complete on the front. Work S&P on the palm to end of round. To make fingerless gloves, proceed to Wristers Only.

Next Round. Front. Right Hand. Work 24 stitches of front in S&P. Cast on 1 stitch with L. **Palm.** Work S&P on palm. Cast on 1 stitch with L (49 stitches). **Left Hand.** Work 24 stitches of front in S&P. Cast on 1 stitch with L. Work S&P on palm. Cast on 1 stitch with L (49 stitches). For Classic Mitten, proceed to Classic Mitten Only.

TRIGGER MITT ONLY

Reserve Trigger Finger Stitches. With Baccalieu facing, at the same edge of the mitten as the thumb place 8 stitches from the front and 8 corresponding stitches from the palm on holders for the trigger finger.

Right Hand. With Baccalieu facing, work in S&P to the gap. Cast on 2 stitches in pattern to bridge the gap. Work in S&P to end of round (35 stitches).

Left Hand. Break yarns. With Baccalieu facing, rejoin yarns. Work S&P on the front and palm to the gap. Cast on 2 stitches to bridge the gap and maintain the pattern. Work in S&P to end of round. Note new beginning of round (35 stitches).

Divide work so that half the stitches are on the front needle and half on the palm needles, with the extra stitch on a palm needle. Do 11 more rounds S&P, or until work reaches the tip of the little finger.

Shape Top. Decreases are made 1 stitch in from the edge at 4 points in the round, positioned as on the toe of a sock. 2 decrease rounds are followed by a round with no decreases, to produce the rounded shape.

Shaping Round 1. Front. K1 in correct colour. SSK with the next colour in the sequence. Resume pattern on next stitch (having made 2 adjacent stitches of the same colour). Work in pattern until 3 stitches remain on the front. K2tog in the same colour as the stitch just made. Work last stitch in correct colour. **Palm.** As front.

Shaping Round 2. Front. K1, SSK in next colour. Work S&P until 3 stitches remain on front. K2tog in next colour, K1. **Palm.** As front. Correct colour sequence is restored.

Shaping Round 3. Work in S&P without decreasing.

Repeat these 3 shaping rounds once more, ending with Round 3 (19 stitches). Break yarns, leaving a 16-inch tail with D.

3-Needle Bind Off. Place stitches of front on a length of waste yarn. Place stitches of palm on waste yarn. Turn mitten inside out to bind off. Return stitches to 2 double-pointed needles. Have the needle with the greater number of stitches nearest you. With a thinner double-pointed needle

for convenience, and D, K1. Then knit together 1 D from the nearest needle with 1 L stitch from the far needle. Pass first stitch on working needle over second stitch. 1 stitch remains on working needle. Continue to knit together 1 stitch of opposite colour from each holding needle, then slipping the first stitch over the second stitch on the working needle, thereby casting off. Repeat until 1 stitch remains. Fasten off and darn ends. Proceed to Trigger Finger and Thumb.

Trigger Finger. Transfer 16 finger stitches to 2 double-pointed needles. **Right Hand.** With front facing, join yarns and work in S&P to gap. Pick up and knit 3 stitches in correct colour order in the finger crease. Note beginning of round. Work in S&P to end of round (19 stitches). **Left Hand.** With front facing, join yarns and work in S&P to the gap. Pick up and knit 3 stitches in correct colour order to bridge the gap. Work S&P to end of round. Note beginning of round (19 stitches).

Work 14 rounds S&P, or until work reaches the tip of the index finger.

Finger Decrease Round 1. (K1 with correct S&P colour. K2tog with next colour. K1 S&P). Repeat to end of round, knitting last 3 stitches in S&P (15 stitches).

Finger Decrease Round 2. (K1, K2tog) in S&P to end of round, working last 3 stitches in S&P. Break yarns, thread through remaining stitches, and secure. Proceed to Thumb.

CLASSIC MITTEN ONLY

Hand. Work 9 more rounds of S&P (or until work reaches the tip of the little finger), ending with Baccalieu facing for next round.

Shape Picket-Fence Top. Decreases are made 1 stitch in from the edge at 4 points in the round, positioned as on the toe of a sock. Decreases are made on every round.

Shaping Round 1. Front. With Baccalieu facing, K1 in correct colour. SSK with the next colour in the sequence. Resume S&P pattern on next stitch (having made 2 adjacent stitches of the same colour). Work in pattern until 3 stitches remain on front. K2tog in the same colour as the stitch just made. Work last stitch in correct colour. **Palm.** As front.

Shaping Round 2. Front. K1, SSK in next colour in the sequence. S&P until 3 stitches remain in front. K2tog in next colour in the sequence, K1. **Palm.** As front. Correct colour sequence is restored.

Repeat these 2 shaping rounds until 9 stitches remain. Break yarns. Thread D into a darning needle and pass through remaining stitches. Pull tight and fasten. Proceed to Thumb.

Thumb. Transfer thumb gusset stitches to 2 needles (8, 7 stitches). Join yarns and work thumb stitches in S&P. Pick up 4 stitches in the crease in correct S&P order (19 stitches). Note beginning of round. Work 12 more rounds in S&P or until work reaches the tip of the thumb.

Thumb Decrease. As Finger Decrease (11 stitches).

Wristers Only. Break L. With D, knit 1 round.

Next Round. Work in (K2, P1) rib, decreasing 6 stitches evenly spaced. Work 2 rounds (K2, P1) ribbing. Cast off in ribbing.

Transfer thumb gusset stitches to 2 needles. With D only, pick up and knit 3 stitches in the crease, knit to end of round (18 stitches). Work 3 rounds (K2, P1) rib. Cast off in rib.

Finishing. Darn ends securely. Press mitten well under a damp cloth. Do not press ribbing.

© Shirley A. Scott 2018

MUG-UP
Long Trigger Mitts for Ladies

DEGREE OF DIFFICULTY: ✳ ✳ TANGLY

Happiness is a mug of tea from water boiled in a flat ass kettle over a fire of blasty boughs. So goes a popular Newfoundland saying. Outdoor lovers enjoy a campfire any time of year, sometimes just for warmth but more often for a hot drink, snack, or full meal. When made from blasty boughs—spruce or fir branches dried to an orange colour—the fire burns fast and hot, needles and twigs crackling cheerfully. If you are wearing your favourite trigger mitts, be careful not to get frankum on them!

In Newfoundland these favourite activities have names. Storm the kettle means building a hot fierce fire to boil the kettle quickly for a speedy cup of tea. No time for food. A mug-up is a hot drink accompanied by a thick slab of homemade bread smothered in butter and molasses, known as lassy bread. A slice of bologna cooked to sizzling brown over the fire on a stick or a few salt capelin roasted in the embers are also delicious local treats. A boil-up, on the other hand, is a full meal deal cooked in one big pot. Jiggs' dinner is a famous example. There's nothin' like a cuppa tea in the woods.

MATERIALS

Briggs and Little Heritage worsted weight yarn, 1 skein Dark (D), 1 skein Light (L). 1 set 3.25 mm double-pointed needles. 1 set 4.00 mm double-pointed needles. Ring markers, darning needle, stitch holders.

SIZE

Ladies' Medium. Circumference: 9 inches (23 cm). Length is measured from cast on to the wrist. Long mitt: 7.75 inches (19 cm). Short mitt: 3.50 inches (9 cm). Length of the hand from beginning of Mug-Up to cast off: 7.25 inches (18.5 cm).

GAUGE

12 stitches x 13 rounds = 2 inches (5 cm) in S&P, using 3.25 mm needles.

MUG-UP CHART (25 stitches x 25 rounds)

Rows (right side, top to bottom): 13, 12, 11, 10, 9, 8, 7, 6, 5, 4, 3, 2, 1

Columns (bottom, left to right): 25, 24, 23, 22, 21, 20, 19, 18, 17, 16, 15, 14, 13, 12, 11, 10, 9, 8, 7, 6, 5, 4, 3, 2, 1

MUG-UP THUMB GUSSET CHART

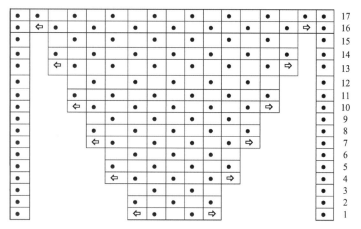

●= K1D   Empty Square= K1L

⇦   Make 1 Left with L   ⇨   Make 1 Right with L

SALT AND PEPPER PATTERN (S&P)

Worked on an odd number of stitches.

Round 1. (K1D, K1L). Repeat to end of round.

Round 2. (K1L, K1D). Repeat to end of round.

Mug-Up Trigger Mitts offer a choice of lengths, standard length or a longer version that reaches just under the elbow. Changes in needle size form the longer version. The body of the mitten is knit with 3.25 mm needles to produce a cozy fit.

Instructions are for both hands unless otherwise stated. Work charts right to left, bottom to top. Always carry D on the left and L on the right to prevent streaks in the work. Please read all instructions before casting on.

Wrist. Long Version. With 4.00 mm needles and D, cast on 40 stitches. Join in a round, being careful not to twist. Work (K3, P1) ribbing for 15 rounds. Join L. Work alternate rounds of L and D (K3, P1) ribbing for 10 rounds (5 L stripes). Break L. With D, work 8 rounds (K3, P1) ribbing. Join L, work 10 rounds of alternating L and D (K3, P1) ribbing (5 L stripes). Change to 3.25 mm needles and, with D, work 16 rounds (K3, P1) ribbing, increasing 8 stitches evenly spaced on final round (48 stitches).

Wrist. Short Version. With 3.25 needles and D, cast on 40 stitches. Join in a round, being careful not to twist. Work 9 rounds of (K3, P1) ribbing. Join L. Work alternate rounds of L and D ribbing for 10 rounds (5 L stripes). Break L. With D, work 8 rounds of ribbing, increasing 8 stitches evenly spaced on the last round (48 stitches).

The Mug-Up (MU) chart vertical repeat is Rounds 1–13, then Rounds 2–13.

Right Mitten. Place stitches on the needles as follows. Needle 1: 25 stitches (front of mitten). Needle 2: 12 stitches. Needle 3: 11 stitches. **Round 1.** Join L. Work Round 1 of MU chart for front of the mitten. Place marker. Work Round 1 of thumb gusset chart (increase round). Place marker. Work Round 1 of S&P to end of round. **Round 2.** Work Round 2 of MU chart. Slip marker. Work Round 2 of thumb gusset chart. Slip marker. Work Round 2 of S&P to end of round.

Continue working successive rounds of MU chart, thumb gusset chart, and S&P until Round 17 is complete. **Round 18.** Work Round 18 of MU chart. Remove marker. K1D over the D outline stitch. Slip 15 thumb gusset stitches on a holder. Cast on 4 stitches in correct colour sequence to bridge the gap. K1D over the final D outline stitch. Remove marker. Work S&P to the end of the round (49 stitches). Thumb gusset is now complete and the 2 D outline stitches

Photo: J. Laaning

have become part of the main section of the mitten. Continue to work successive rounds of MU chart on the front of the mitten and S&P on the palm until Round 25 is complete. Work 2 rounds S&P.

Right Index Finger. Break yarns. Transfer 7 stitches from the end of needle 1 to another 3.25 mm needle. Place the first 7 stitches from needle 2 on another needle. Slip the remaining 35 stitches from the front and palm on a holder. Keeping S&P correct, rejoin yarns and knit 7 stitches on needle 1. Knit 7 stitches on needle 2 in S&P. With a third needle cast on 5 stitches in correct colour sequence to bridge the gap. Join these stitches in a round (19 stitches). Work 15 rounds or desired length in S&P. Break L. With D, K2tog to last 3 stitches. K3 tog. Break D, leaving a tail. Thread through remaining stitches, pull up and fasten securely.

Right Hand. Slip the 35 stitches from holder to 3 needles. Needle 1: 18 (front of mitten). Needles 2 and 3 share 17 stitches for the palm. With Mug-Up facing, rejoin yarns.

Frankum: Also frankgum. The hardened resin of a spruce tree, often used for chewing.

—DICTIONARY OF NEWFOUNDLAND ENGLISH

Work in S&P to index finger. Pick up and knit 4 stitches in the correct colour sequence at the base of the index finger. Continue in S&P to end of round (39 stitches). Work 14 more rounds of S&P. Slip 1 stitch from the beginning of needle 2 to the end of needle 1 (19 stitches on needle 1; needles 2 and 3 share the 20 palm stitches). Proceed to Shape Top.

Left Hand. Arrange stitches as follows. Needle 1: 25 stitches (front of mitten). Needle 2: 12 stitches. Needle 3: 11 stitches. **Round 1.** Join L. Work Round 1 of MU chart on needle 1. Work Round 1 of S&P on needle 2. Work S&P to last 5 stitches of needle 3. Place marker. Work Round 1 of thumb gusset chart (increase round). Place marker. **Round 2.** Work Round 2 of MU chart on front of mitten. Work S&P to marker. Slip marker. Work Round 2 of thumb gusset chart. Slip marker. Left hand thumb gusset is now positioned.

Continue to work successive rounds of MU chart on the front, S&P to the marker, and thumb gusset chart to the end of Round 17. **Round 18.** Work Round 18 of MU chart. Work S&P to marker. Remove marker. K1 in correct colour sequence. Slip 15 thumb gusset stitches on a holder. Cast on 4 stitches in correct colour sequence to bridge the gap. K1D over the final D outline stitch. Remove marker (49 stitches). Thumb gusset is now complete. Continue to work successive rounds of MU chart on the front of the mitten and S&P on the palm until Round 25 is complete. Work 2 rounds S&P.

Left Index Finger. Work S&P on first 7 stitches of needle 1. Slip the next 35 stitches onto a holder. 7 stitches remain on needle 3. With front facing, and using another 3.25 mm needle, cast on 5 stitches in correct colour sequence to bridge the gap. Work 7 stitches in S&P on needle 3. Join these stitches in a round (19 stitches). Work 15 rounds or desired length in S&P. Break L. With D, K2tog to last 3 stitches. K3 tog. Break D, leaving a tail. Thread through remaining stitches, pull up and fasten securely.

Left Hand. With Mug-Up facing, slip 18 stitches from holder to needle 1. Place first 10 palm stitches on needle 2. Slip the remaining 7 palm stitches to needle 3. Rejoin yarns. Pick up and knit 4 stitches in correct colour sequence at the base of the index finger (39 stitches). With Mug-Up facing, work 13 more rounds of S&P. Work in S&P until 1 stitch remains on needle 1. Slip this stitch to the beginning of needle 2. Work S&P to the end of the round. (Needle 1: 19 stitches, needles 2 and 3 share the 20 palm stitches.) Proceed to Shape Top.

Shape Top. On odd numbered rounds, decreasing will create 2 adjacent stitches in the same colour. On the following even numbered rounds, these stitches will be worked together, restoring the correct colour sequence. Decreases are made 1 stitch in from the edge of the needles at 4 points in the round.

Shaping Round 1. Needle 1. K1 in correct colour. SSK with the next colour in the sequence. Resume pattern on the next stitch (having made 2 adjacent stitches of the same colour). Work in S&P until 3 stitches remain on needle. K2tog in the same colour as the stitch just made. Work last stitch in the correct S&P colour. **Needle 2.** K1. SSK as above. Work in pattern to the end of the needle. **Needle 3.** Work in pattern until 3 stitches remain in round. K2tog in the same colour as the stitch just made. K1 in correct colour. **Shaping Round 2.** Work SSK and K2tog decreases at the same points as the previous round. Colour sequence will be restored. Repeat these 2 shaping rounds until 15 stitches remain. Break yarns, leaving a D tail approximately 12 inches (30 cm) long and a short L tail sufficient for darning. Cast off using 3-needle bind off.

3-Needle Bind Off. Place stitches from the front of the mitten on a length of waste yarn. Place the stitches of the palm on another length of waste yard. Turn the mitten inside out to work the bind off on the wrong side. Return the stitches from the yarn onto 2 thinner double-pointed needles for convenience. Hold these needles parallel to one another. Have the needle with the greater number of stitches nearest you. With a third needle, and using the long tail of D, K1 from the holding needle nearest you. Then knit 1 stitch from the front needle with 1 stitch of the opposite colour from the back needle (2 stitches on the working needle). Pass first stitch on the working needle over the second stitch to cast it off. 1 stitch remains on the working needle. Continue to knit together 1 stitch from the front and back needles and slipping the first stitch over the second stitch on the working needle to cast off. Repeat until 1 stitch remains. Break yarns. Thread through remaining stitch. Draw up and fasten securely.

Thumb. Slip 15 thumb gusset stitches from holder to 2 needles. Rejoin yarns. With a third needle pick up and knit 6 stitches in correct colour sequence at the base of the thumb (21 stitches). Work 13 rounds or desired length in S&P. Break L. Using D, K2tog until 3 stitches remain. K3 tog. Break D. Draw through remaining stitches and fasten securely.

Finishing. Carefully darn in all ends and trim neatly. Press under a damp cloth, omitting ribbing.

© Christine LeGrow 2018

CORNER BOY
Gloves for Men

DEGREE OF DIFFICULTY: ✳✳ TANGLY

Corner boys were street-smart fellows who spent their leisure in conversation and observation on the busy corners of St. John's. Their tiny territories were fiercely guarded. Scorned by baymen and considered layabouts by many fellow townies, they worked hard to present a louche urban style when loitering in their places of safety. They played the sport of casually getting and spending money. They perfected the fine art of telling a yarn. From their corner strongholds they excelled in quick appraisal of the passing scene. These distinctive gloves are for all fine fellows who champion the streetwise way of life in town.

MATERIALS

1 set of 4.00 mm double-pointed needles. 1 skein Briggs and Little Regal 2-ply worsted weight wool in Dark (D), 1 skein in Light (L). Ring markers, lengths of yarn for stitch holders.

SIZE

Men's Medium. Circumference: 9 inches (23 cm). Length: 11 inches (28 cm) from cast on to tip of middle finger. Thumb: 2.25 inches (6 cm). Index finger: 2.75 inches (7 cm). Middle finger: 3 inches (7.5 cm). Ring finger: 2.75 inches (7 cm). Baby finger: 2.5 inches (6.5 cm). Length of thumb and fingers is adjustable.

GAUGE

24 stitches x 28 rows = 4 inches (10 cm).

SALT AND PEPPER PATTERN (S&P)

Worked over an odd number of stitches.
Round 1. (K1D, K1L). Repeat to end of round.
Round 2. (K1L, K1D). Repeat to end of round.

By the men's glances at the city dwellers or "corner boys," no love seemed lost between them.

—GEORGE ALLAN ENGLAND, *VIKINGS OF THE ICE*

CORNER BOY CHART (6 stitches x 8 rows)

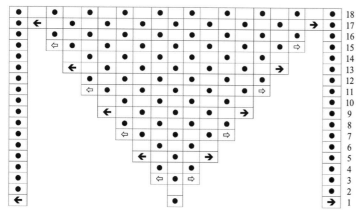

THUMB GUSSET CHART

- • K1D
- → Make 1 Right with D
- ⇦ Make 1 Left with L

Empty square = K1L
- ← Make 1 Left with D
- ⇨ Make 1 Right with L

Work charts from right to left, bottom to top. Always carry D on the left and L on the right to prevent streaks in the work. Instructions apply to both hands unless otherwise stated.

Wrist. With D, cast on 42 stitches. Divide evenly on 3 needles and join in a circle, being careful not to twist. Work 27 rounds of (K2, P1) rib in a striped pattern of your choice. **Next Round.** With D, knit, increasing 12 stitches evenly spaced (54 stitches). Arrange work on needles 27, 14, 13 stitches.

Round 1. Join L, and keeping D ahead (i.e., on the left) throughout, work Round 1 of Corner Boy chart 4 times, then work stitches 1–3. These 27 stitches form the front of the glove. **Right Hand.** K1D, K1L. Place marker. Work Round 1 of thumb gusset chart. Place marker. (K1L, K1D) to end of round. These stitches form the palm. **Left Hand.** (K1D, K1L) until 3 stitches remain in round. Place marker. Work Round 1 of thumb gusset chart. Place marker. K1L, K1D.

This sets up the Corner Boy pattern on the front and S&P on the palm and places the point of the thumb gusset with its 2 D outline stitches between the markers.

Round 2. Front. Work Round 2 of Corner Boy chart. **Palm.** Work in S&P to marker. Slip marker. Work Round 2 of thumb gusset chart to marker. Slip marker. Work in S&P to end of round. Note that beginning with gusset Round 3, gusset increases are made within the outline stitches on every second round, in the colour indicated.

Continue working successive rounds of Corner Boy on the front of the glove, S&P on the palm, and the thumb gusset within the markers until gusset Round 18 is complete, finishing the row in S&P (19 gusset stitches between markers). **Next Round.** Work in patterns as established to marker. Remove marker. Place 19 gusset stitches on a holder. Remove marker. Make 1 with correct S&P colour to bridge the gap. Work in pattern to end of round (54 stitches).

Continue working Corner Boy on the front and S&P on the palm until 28 rounds of Corner Boy are complete, ending with Round 4 of the chart. Finish the palm in S&P. Beginning with K1D, work 1 round of S&P on the front. Cast on 1 stitch with L. S&P on palm (55 stitches). **Right Hand Only.** Break yarns.

Dressed in their very best.
Photo: by permission of R. Abbott

DIVIDE FOR FINGERS

Cut 6 lengths of waste yarn to hold finger stitches.

Right Hand. Front. With Corner Boy facing, and beginning at the right edge of the glove, put 6 stitches on holder for baby finger. Put next 7 stitches on holder for ring finger. Put next 7 stitches on holder for middle finger. **Palm.** Put corresponding 6 stitches on holder for baby finger, 7 stitches for ring finger, 7 stitches for middle finger. 15 stitches remain on needles for index finger.

Left Hand. Front. With Corner Boy facing, and beginning at the left edge of the glove, put 6 stitches on holder for baby finger. Put next 7 stitches on holder for ring finger. Place next 7 stitches on holder for middle finger. **Palm.** Put corresponding 6 stitches on holder for baby finger, 7 stitches for ring finger, 7 stitches for middle finger. 15 stitches remain on needles for index finger.

Right Index Finger. With Corner Boy facing, rejoin yarns. Work 15 stitches in S&P. Cast on 6 stitches in correct S&P sequence (21 stitches). Divide work on 3 needles and join in a circle. Note beginning of round. Work 15 more rounds of S&P, or until work reaches the tip of the finger. Work Finger Decrease Rounds 1 and 2.

Right Middle Finger. Transfer 7 stitches from front and 7 from palm to double-pointed needles. With Corner Boy facing, rejoin yarns and work front stitches in S&P. Pick up and knit 3 stitches in correct colour order from the base of the index finger. Work palm stitches in S&P. Cast on 4 stitches in correct S&P order (21 stitches). Divide work on 3 needles and join in a circle. Note beginning of round. Work 18 more rounds in S&P, or until work reaches the tip of the finger. Work Finger Decrease Rounds 1 and 2.

Right Ring Finger. Transfer 7 stitches from front and 7 from palm to double-pointed needles. With Corner Boy facing, rejoin yarns and work front stitches in S&P. Pick up and knit 3 stitches in correct colour order from the base of the middle finger. Work palm stitches in S&P. Cast on 4 stitches in correct S&P order (21 stitches). Divide work on 3 needles and join in a circle. Note beginning of round. Work 15 more rounds in S&P, or until work reaches the tip of the finger. Work Finger Decrease Rounds 1 and 2.

Right Baby Finger. Transfer 6 stitches from front and 6 from palm to double-pointed needles. With Corner Boy facing, rejoin yarns and work front stitches in S&P. Pick up and knit 7 stitches in correct colour order from the base of the ring finger. Work palm stitches in S&P (19 stitches). Divide work on 3 needles and join in a circle. Note beginning

of round. Work 13 more rounds in S&P, or until work reaches the tip of the finger. Work Finger Decrease Rounds 1 and 2.

Left Index Finger. With Corner Boy facing, work 8 front stitches in S&P. Cast on 6 stitches in correct S&P order. Work 7 palm stitches in S&P. Divide work on 3 needles and join in a circle (21 stitches). Note beginning of round. Work 15 more rounds of S&P, or until work reaches the tip of the finger. Work Finger Decrease Rounds 1 and 2.

Left Middle Finger. Transfer 7 stitches from front and 7 from palm to double-pointed needles. With Corner Boy facing, rejoin yarns and work front stitches in S&P. Cast on 4 stitches in correct S&P order. Work 7 palm stitches in S&P. Pick up and knit 3 stitches in correct colour order from the base of the index finger (21 stitches). Divide work on 3 needles and join in a circle. Note beginning of round. Work 18 more rounds in S&P, or until work reaches the tip of the finger. Work Finger Decrease Rounds 1 and 2.

Left Ring Finger. Transfer 7 stitches from front and 7 from palm to double-pointed needles. With Corner Boy facing, rejoin yarns and work front stitches in S&P. Cast on 4 stitches in correct S&P order. Work palm stitches in S&P. Pick up and knit 3 stitches in correct colour order from the base of the middle finger (21 stitches). Divide work on 3 needles and join in a circle. Note beginning of round. Work 15 more rounds in S&P, or until work reaches the tip of the finger. Work Finger Decrease Rounds 1 and 2.

Left Baby Finger. Transfer 6 stitches from front and 6 from palm to double-pointed needles. With Corner Boy facing, rejoin yarns and work front stitches in S&P. Work palm stitches in S&P. Pick up and knit 7 stitches in correct colour order from the base of the ring finger (19 stitches). Divide work on 3 needles and join in a circle. Note beginning of round. Work 13 more rounds in S&P, or until work reaches the tip of the finger. Work Finger Decrease Rounds 1 and 2.

Finger Decrease Round 1. (K1 with correct colour in S&P sequence, K2tog with next colour in sequence, K1 in S&P). Repeat to end of round, working any leftover stitches in S&P. Adjacent stitches in the same colour will be eliminated in the next round. **Finger Decrease Round 2.** (K1 with correct S&P colour, K2tog with next colour in S&P sequence), working any leftover stitches in S&P. Break yarns. Thread through remaining stitches and secure.

Thumb. Transfer thumb stitches from holder to 2 double-pointed needles. Rejoin yarns and knit these stitches in S&P. With another needle, pick up and knit 2 stitches in S&P at the base of the thumb (21 stitches). Work 13 rounds more in S&P, or desired length. Work Finger Decrease Rounds 1 and 2.

Finishing. Darn ends securely. Press well, omitting ribbing.

LITTLE CORNER BOY
Mittens for Youngsters

DEGREE OF DIFFICULTY: ✳ ✳ TANGLY

Young boys from the downtown area of St. John's had little in common with their older counterparts, the big corner boys. These young boys were full of energy and youthful ambition. They ran instead of walked, stopping only when they arrived at a favourite corner. There were many popular corners in the old city. A famous one was the intersection of Duckworth and Prescott Streets, with the ever-present traffic cop on duty. He expertly directed vehicles and pedestrians alike across this busy intersection. A wave of his hands and a high-pitched whistle did the job. It is certain many little corner boys grew up to become members of the Royal Newfoundland Constabulary because of the inspirational cop on this corner.

MATERIALS

Briggs and Little Heritage worsted weight wool, oddments of Dark (D), Light (L), and Contrast (C) colours. 1 set of 3.50 mm double-pointed needles. 1 set of 4.00 mm double-pointed needles. Ring markers, darning needle, stitch holders or lengths of waste yarn.

SIZE

To fit a youngster approximately 4 to 6 years old. Circumference: 7.25 inches (18.5 cm). Length measured from the beginning of the Little Corner Boy pattern to cast off: 6.5 inches (16.5 cm).

GAUGE

11 stitches x 13 rounds = 2 inches (5 cm) worked over Little Corner Boy pattern, using 4.00 mm needles.

SALT AND PEPPER PATTERN (S&P)

Worked on an odd number of stitches.

Round 1. (K1D, K1L). Repeat to end of round.

Round 2. (K1L, K1D). Repeat to end of round.

LITTLE CORNER BOY

Right Hand

4	3	2	1	
●	●	◊	◊	4
●	●	◊	◊	3
		●	●	2
		●	●	1

4 3 2 1

LITTLE CORNER BOY

Left Hand

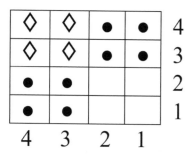

4	3	2	1	
◊	◊	●	●	4
◊	◊	●	●	3
●	●			2
●	●			1

4 3 2 1

Horizontal repeat: 4 times = 16 stitches

Vertical repeat: 5 times = 20 rounds

THUMB GUSSET CHART

- ● K1D
- ◊ K1 Contrast
- → Make 1 Right with C
- ⇨ Make 1 Right with L
- Empty square = K1L
- ← Make 1 Left with C
- ⇦ Make 1 Left with L

Little Corner Boy mittens are mirror images. Three colours are used; therefore, the D and L are placed nearest the thumb gusset side on both mittens. The thumb gussets are worked with a D outline stitch on each side. Always carry D to the left (ahead) and L and C to the right to prevent streaks in the work.

Wrist. With 3.50 mm double-pointed needles and D, cast on 33 stitches. Join in round, being careful not to twist. Work (K2, P1) rib for 17 rounds, increasing 4 stitches evenly spaced on the last round. Change to 4.00 mm double-pointed needles. Work charts from right to left, bottom to top.

Right Hand. Round 1. Join L. Keeping 16 stitches on the first needle for the front of the mitten, work Round 1 of Right Hand LCB (RHLCB) chart on needle 1. Place marker. (K1D, K1L, K1D, K1L, K1D). These 5 stitches are Round 1 on the thumb gusset chart and form the base of the thumb gusset. Place marker. Work Round 1 of S&P to end of round.

Round 2. Increase Round. Work Round 2 of RHLCB chart. Slip marker. Work Round 2 of thumb gusset chart. Slip marker. Work Round 2 of S&P to end of round.

Round 3. Drop L and join C. Work Round 3 of RHLCB chart. Slip marker. Work Round 3 of thumb gusset chart. Slip marker. Work Round 1 of S&P to end of round.

Continue in this established manner, having the front of the mitten in LCB pattern, thumb gusset stitches between the markers, and S&P on palm until there are 11 stitches between the 2 D outline stitches and Round 12 is complete.

Next Round. Work Round 13 of LCB chart. Remove marker. K1L over D outline stitch. Slip the 11 thumb gusset stitches on a length of waste yarn. Cast on 3 stitches in the correct colour sequence to bridge the gap. Remove marker. K1L over D outline stitch. Work S&P on the palm, completing the round. The thumb gusset is now complete (37 stitches).

Continue until 20 rounds of LCB chart are complete on the front of the mitten. Work palm in S&P pattern to the end of the round. Break C. Slip 2 stitches from the beginning of the second needle onto the end of the first needle. There are now 18 stitches on the first needle (front of mitten), the second and third needles share the 19 stitches of the palm. Proceed to Both Mittens.

Left Mitten. Round 1. Place marker. Work Round 1 of thumb gusset chart. Place marker. Work Round 1 of Left Hand LCB (LHLCB) chart. Work Round 1 S&P to end of round. **Round 2. Increase Round.** Slip marker. Work Round 2 of thumb gusset chart. Slip marker. Work Round 2 of LHLCB chart. Work S&P on the palm. **Round 3.** Place L to the right to use in Round 13. Join C. Slip marker. Work Round 3 of thumb gusset chart. Slip marker. Work Round 3 of LHLCB chart. Work S&P on the palm.

Continue in this established pattern, having the thumb gusset at the start of the round, LHLCB chart (front of the mitten) and S&P on the palm, until Round 12 is complete.

Round 13. Remove marker. K1L over the D outline stitch. Slip the 11 thumb gusset stitches on waste yarn. Cast on 3 stitches in correct colour sequence to bridge the gap. K1L over the D outline stitch. Work Round 13 of LHLCB on the front of the mitten and S&P on the palm. Work until Round 20 of LHLCB chart is complete. Work S&P until 2 stitches remain in the round. Break C. Slip these last 2 stitches from the end of the third needle onto the beginning of the first needle.

The stitches are now arranged as follows. Needle 1: 18 stitches for the front of the mitten. Needle 2 and needle 3 share the 19 palm stitches.

Both Mittens. Work 4 rounds S&P, or desired length, ending with Round 2 of S&P.

Shape Top. On odd numbered rounds, decreasing will create 2 adjacent stitches of the same colour. On the following even numbered decrease rounds, these stitches will be worked together, restoring the correct colour sequence. Decreases are made 1 stitch in from the edge of the needle at 4 points in the round.

Shaping Round 1. Needle 1. K1 in correct colour. SSK with the next colour in the sequence. Resume pattern on next stitch (having made 2 adjacent stitches of the same colour) and work until 3 stitches remain before the end of the needle. K2tog in the same colour as the stitch just made. Work last stitch in correct colour. **Needle 2.** K1. SSK with next colour in sequence. Work in pattern to the end of the

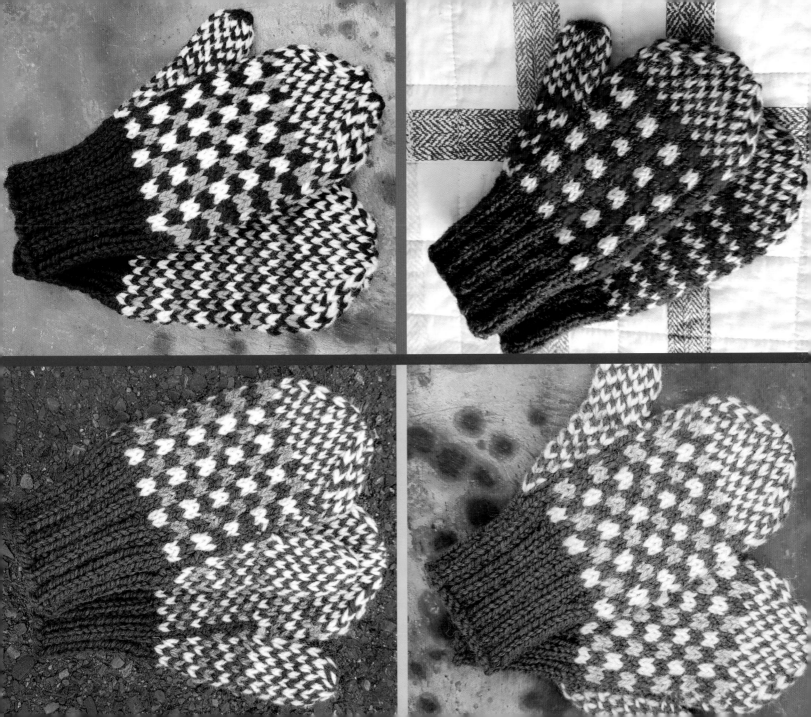

needle. **Needle 3.** Pattern until 3 stitches remain before the end of round. K2tog in the same colour as the stitch just made. K1 in correct colour. **Shaping Round 2.** Work SSK and K2tog decreases in S&P at the same points as the previous round. Correct colour sequence will be restored. Repeat these 2 shaping rounds until 13 stitches remain.

Break yarns, leaving a D tail approximately 12 inches (30 cm) long to complete the bind off and a short L tail sufficient for darning. Cast off using 3-needle bind off.

3-Needle Bind Off. Place the stitches from the front of the mitten on a length of waste yarn. Place the stitches of the palm on another length of waste yarn. Turn the mitten inside out to work the bind off on the wrong side. Return the stitches from the waste yarn onto 2 thinner double-pointed needles for convenience. Hold these needles parallel to one another with the needle with the greater number of stitches nearest you. With a third needle, and using the long tail of D, K1 from the holding needle nearest you. Then knit 1 stitch from the front needle together with 1 stitch of the opposite colour from the back needle. There are now 2 stitches on the working needle. Pass first stitch on the working needle over the second stitch to cast it off. 1 stitch remains on the working needle. Continue to knit together 1 stitch from the front and back needles and slipping the first stitch over the second stitch on the working needle to cast off. Repeat until 1 stitch remains. Fasten off and darn ends.

Thumb. Slip 11 stitches from the waste yarn to two 3.50 mm needles. With a third needle pick up and knit 4 stitches in the correct colour sequence at the base of the thumb. Keeping S&P sequence correct, work 9 rounds, or desired length. Break L. With D, K2tog to last stitch, K1D. Break yarn, leaving a tail 6 inches long. Thread through a darning needle, slip though remaining loops and fasten off securely.

Finishing. Darn in all ends neatly. Carefully press under a damp cloth, omitting ribbing.

GRENFELL
Trigger Mitts for Men

DEGREE OF DIFFICULTY: ✳ ✳ ✳ OVER THE WHARF

The Grenfell Mission was the primary source of medical care for Labrador and northern Newfoundland for nearly a century. In 1892 a young British medical missionary named Wilfred Grenfell made his first voyage to Newfoundland and Labrador. He was deeply moved by both the suffering and the self-reliance of its people. He subsequently built and developed a large number of hospitals and other services in the area. "The Industrial," as the handcrafts division of the Mission was known, was established to encourage alternative sources of income. It created a significant measure of pride as well as prosperity. Weaving, sewing, knitting, and woodworking were among the skills nourished by the Mission. Known for highest standards of quality and workmanship, the legacy of The Industrial remains strong today. This very sophisticated mitten was often seen in displays of Grenfell handiwork.

SIZE

Men's Large. Circumference: 10 inches (25 cm). Length of mitten from beginning of Grenfell pattern: 8.5 inches (18 cm).

Trigger finger: 3.5 inches (9 cm). Thumb: 3.25 inches (9 cm). Length of hand, thumb, and trigger finger is adjustable.

MATERIALS

2 shades of Briggs and Little Regal 2-ply worsted weight wool, 1 skein in Dark (D), 1 skein in Light (L). 1 set of 4.00 mm double-pointed needles. 2 thinner double-pointed needles for 3-needle bind off only. Ring markers.

GAUGE

24 stitches x 28 rows = 4 inches (10 cm).

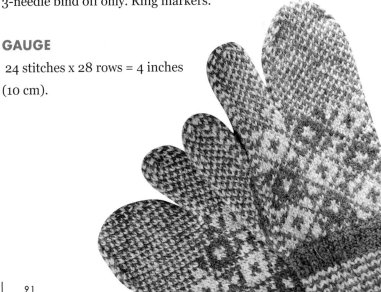

GRENFELL CHART (29 stitches x 29 rows)

	29	28	27	26	25	24	23	22	21	20	19	18	17	16	15	14	13	12	11	10	9	8	7	6	5	4	3	2	1
29		•		•		•		•		•		•		•		•		•		•		•		•		•		•	
19		•	•	•		•		•	•	•				•		•				•	•	•		•		•	•	•	
18	•	•	•		•	•	•			•	•		•				•			•	•		•	•	•		•	•	•
17		•		•	•	•	•		•			•					•			•		•		•	•	•		•	
16	•		•	•	•		•	•	•				•			•			•		•	•	•			•	•	•	•
15		•	•	•						•	•	•					•			•	•			•		•	•	•	
14	•		•	•	•		•	•	•		•		•					•		•	•	•			•	•	•		•
13		•		•	•	•	•		•		•				•			•		•	•	•				•	•	•	
12	•	•	•		•	•	•				•		•		•			•	•	•			•		•	•	•		•
11		•	•	•		•		•	•	•		•		•						•	•			•		•	•	•	
10	•			•		•			•	•	•		•		•	•	•						•		•				•
9			•			•			•	•		•	•	•		•	•		•			•				•			
8	•		•				•		•		•	•	•	•	•		•		•		•				•				•
7		•			•			•		•	•	•		•	•	•		•				•				•			
6	•		•	•	•					•	•	•		•	•	•		•					•	•	•				•
5		•			•			•		•	•	•		•	•	•		•				•				•			
4	•		•				•		•		•	•	•		•	•		•		•				•		•			•
3			•			•			•	•		•	•	•		•	•				•				•				
2	•			•		•			•	•	•		•		•	•						•		•		•			•
1		•		•		•		•		•		•		•		•		•		•		•		•		•		•	

29 28 27 26 25 24 23 22 21 20 19 18 17 16 15 14 13 12 11 10 9 8 7 6 5 4 3 2 1

GRENFELL THUMB GUSSET CHART

- ● K1D
- → Make 1 Right with D
- ⇦ Make 1 Left with L

- Empty square = K1L
- ← Make 1 Left with D
- ⇨ Make 1 Right with L

SALT AND PEPPER PATTERN (S&P)

Worked over an odd number of stitches.

Round 1. (K1D, K1L). Repeat to end of round.

Round 2. (K1L, K1D). Repeat to end of round.

Instructions are for both hands unless otherwise indicated. Work charts from right to left, bottom to top. Always carry D on the left and L on the right to prevent streaks in the work.

With D, cast on 45 stitches. Join in a circle, being careful not to twist. Work 27 rounds in (K2, P1) ribbing in a striped pattern of your choice. **Next Round.** Knit, increasing 14 stitches evenly spaced (59 stitches). Arrange 29 stitches on needle 1 for the front of the mitten. Divide remaining stitches on needles 2 and 3 for the palm.

Round 1. Front. Always carrying D ahead, join L and work Round 1 of the Grenfell chart for the front of the mitten (29 stitches). **Palm. Right Hand.** K1D, K1L. Place marker. Make 1 right-leaning stitch with D. K1D. Make 1 left-leaning stitch with D. Place marker. Work (K1L, K1D) to end of round. There will be 3 D stitches between markers. **Palm. Left Hand.** (K1D, K1L) until 4 stitches remain in round. Place marker. M1R with D. K1D. M1L with D. Place marker. K1L, K1D, K1L. There will be 3 D stitches between markers.

This sets up 29 Grenfell pattern stitches on the front of the mitten and S&P stitches on the palm, with the thumb gusset stitches between markers. The gusset is outlined with D stitches inside the markers.

Round 2. Front. Work Round 2 of the Grenfell chart. **Palm.** Work S&P to marker. Slip marker. Work Round 2 of thumb gusset chart to next marker. Slip marker. Work S&P to end of round.

Continue in patterns as established, working successive rows of thumb gusset chart between markers until Round 18 of Grenfell and thumb gusset is complete. Work S&P to end of round. There will be 19 gusset stitches between markers.

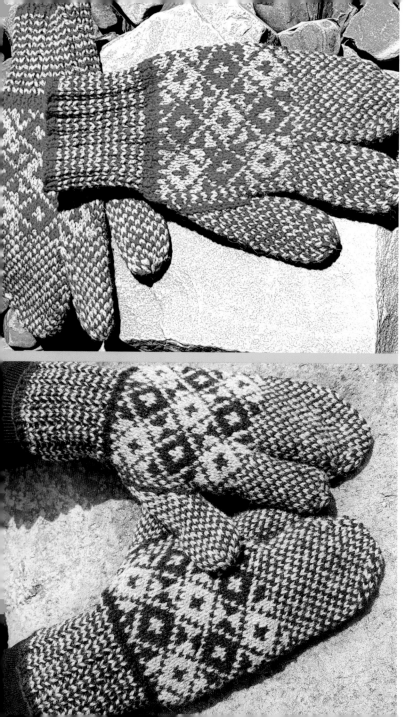

Next Round. Front. Work Round 19 of Grenfell. **Palm.** Work S&P to marker. Remove marker. Place gusset stitches on a holder. Cast on 1 stitch with D to bridge the gap. Remove marker. Work S&P to end of round (59 stitches). **Next Round.** Work Round 2 of Grenfell on front, S&P on palm.

Continue working successive rows of Grenfell on the front of the mitten and S&P on the palm until Grenfell Round 10 is complete, S&P on palm. **Next Round.** Work Round 29 of Grenfell on front, S&P on palm.

Reserve Trigger Finger Stitches. Use lengths of waste yarn for stitch holders. **Right Hand.** With Grenfell facing, work 20 stitches in S&P. Place next 9 stitches of front on holder for trigger finger. Place corresponding 9 stitches of palm on holder for trigger finger. Cast on 2 stitches in correct S&P order to bridge the gap, work S&P to end of round (43 stitches).

Left Hand. Break yarns. Place first 9 stitches of Grenfell on holder for trigger finger. Place the corresponding 9 stitches of palm on holder for trigger finger. With Grenfell facing, rejoin yarns and, beginning with K1L, work S&P on front, S&P on palm. Cast on 2 stitches in S&P to bridge the gap (43 stitches).

Both Hands. Work 15 rounds more in S&P, ending with Grenfell facing for the next round. Arrange stitches 21, 11, 11.

Shape Top. Note that some shaping rounds produce 2 adjacent stitches in the same colour at 4 points in the round. These will be eliminated in the following round.

Shaping Round 1. Front. K1 with correct S&P colour. SSK with the next colour in the sequence. Work S&P until 3 stitches remain on front needle. K2tog with the same colour as the stitch just made. K1 in correct colour of S&P. **Palm.** Work as for front (4 stitches decreased).

Shaping Round 2. Front. K1 in S&P. SSK with next colour in the sequence. S&P to last 3 stitches of front. K2tog with next colour in the sequence. K1 in S&P. **Palm.** Work as for front (4 stitches decreased).

Shaping Round 3. Work in S&P without decreasing.

Repeat shaping Rounds 1–3 twice (19 stitches). Break L, leaving a 3-inch tail. Break D, leaving a 14-inch tail.

3-Needle Bind Off. The hand is finished with a 3-needle bind off on the wrong side of the work.

Place stitches of the front on a length of waste yarn. Place stitches of the palm on another length of yarn. Turn mitten inside out to work bind off on the wrong side, using the long tail of D.

Return stitches on holders to 2 thinner double-pointed

Photo: J. Laaning

needles for easier working. Hold these needles parallel to one another, the needle with the larger number of stitches nearest you. With a third double-pointed needle and D, K1 from the holding needle nearest you. Then knit 1 stitch from this needle together with 1 stitch of the opposite colour from the back needle. You now have 2 stitches on the working needle. Pass first stitch on working needle over second stitch to cast it off. 1 stitch remains on working needle. Continue to knit together 1 stitch from front and back needles and slipping the first stitch over second stitch on the working needle to cast off. Repeat until 1 stitch remains. Fasten off and darn ends.

Trigger Finger. Transfer 9 stitches from front holder to a double-pointed needle. Place 9 stitches from the palm on a double-pointed needle.

Right Trigger Finger. With Grenfell facing, rejoin yarns. Beginning with K1D, work stitches on front and palm in S&P. With another double-pointed needle, pick up and knit 5 stitches in correct S&P sequence from the base of the hand (23 stitches).

Left Trigger Finger. With Grenfell facing, rejoin yarns. Beginning with K1D, work 9 stitches of front in S&P. Pick up and knit 5 stitches in correct colour sequence from base of hand. Work 9 palm stitches in S&P (23 stitches).

Both Hands. Note beginning of round. Divide stitches on 3 double-pointed needles and work 16 rounds more of S&P, or until work reaches the tip of the index finger.

Finger Decrease Round 1. (K1 with correct colour in S&P sequence, K2tog with next colour in sequence, K1 in S&P), repeat to end of round, working any remaining stitches in S&P. Adjacent stitches in the same colour will be eliminated in the next round.

Finger Decrease Round 2. (K1 with correct S&P colour, K2tog with next colour in S&P sequence), repeat to end of round, working any remaining stitches in S&P. Break yarns. Thread through remaining stitches and secure.

Thumb. Transfer thumb stitches from holder to 2 double-pointed needles. Rejoin yarns and knit these stitches in S&P. With another needle, pick up and knit 4 stitches in S&P at the base of the thumb (23 stitches). Note beginning of round. Work 15 rounds more in S&P, or until work reaches the tip of the thumb. Decrease as for fingers.

Finishing. Darn ends securely. Press lightly under a damp cloth, omitting ribbing.

© Shirley A. Scott 2018

SPRING ICE
Trigger Mitts for Ladies

DEGREE OF DIFFICULTY: ✳ ✳ TANGLY

Signs of spring are different here. In Newfoundland this gentle, fertile season is harsh and tumultuous. Great expanses of pack ice drift southward on the cold Labrador Current. When forced by wind and tide into bays and coves along the coastline, they bring a halt to movement. We are icebound until the shipping lanes are opened and a change of wind drives the heaving mass back out to sea. Marine mammals may be trapped among the floes. Polar bears wander into shore communities. Huge icebergs break away and drift slowly southward into warmth and oblivion. Despite such disruptions and dangers spring in Newfoundland also brings unsurpassed scenes of rare, ethereal beauty. These mitts suggest the beauty of the sea ice that hugs our shores in springtime. You may also know this venerable pattern as Tumbling Blocks.

MATERIALS

Two shades of Briggs and Little Regal 2-ply worsted weight wool, 1 skein Dark (D), 1 skein Light (L). 1 set of 4.00 mm double-pointed needles. 2 thinner double-pointed needles for 3-needle bind off only. Ring markers.

SIZE

Ladies' Medium. Length is adjustable. Circumference: 7.5 inches (19.5 cm). Length of mitten from beginning of Spring Ice pattern: 7 inches (18 cm). Trigger finger: 2.75 inches (7 cm). Thumb: 2.25 inches (5.5 cm). Length of hand, thumb, and trigger finger is adjustable.

GAUGE

24 stitches and 28 rows = 4 inches (10 cm).

SALT AND PEPPER PATTERN (S&P)

Worked over an odd number of stitches.

Round 1. (K1D, K1L). Repeat to end of round.

Round 2. (K1L, K1D). Repeat to end of round.

SPRING ICE CHART (8 stitches x 14 rows)

8	7	6	5	4	3	2	1	
	●		●		●		●	14
●		●	●			●		13
	●	●	●				●	12
●	●	●	●					11
●	●	●		●				10
●	●		●		●			9
●		●		●		●		8
	●		●		●		●	7
		●		●		●	●	6
			●		●	●	●	5
			●	●	●	●		4
●			●	●	●			3
	●		●	●			●	2
●		●		●		●		1

SPRING ICE THUMB GUSSET CHART

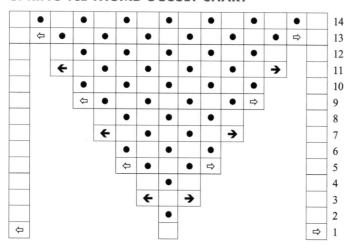

- ● K1D
- → Make 1 Right with D
- ⇦ Make 1 Left with L
- Empty square = K1L
- ← Make 1 Left with D
- ⇨ Make 1 Right with L

Work charts from right to left, bottom to top, beginning at the bottom right. Always carry D in the left hand (i.e., ahead) and L in the right to prevent streaks in the work. Instructions are for both hands unless otherwise indicated.

Wrist. With D, cast on 36 stitches. Join in a circle, being careful not to twist. Work 26 rounds in (K2, P1) ribbing in a striped pattern of your choice. **Next Round.** With D, knit, increasing 11 stitches evenly spaced (47 stitches). Arrange 24 stitches on needle 1 for the front of the mitten. Divide remaining stitches on needles 2 and 3 for the palm.

Round 1. Front. Always carrying D ahead, join L and work Round 1 of Spring Ice chart 3 times for the front of the mitten (24 stitches). **Palm. Right Hand.** K1L, K1D. Place marker. Make 1 right-leaning stitch with L. K1. Make 1 left-leaning stitch with L. Place marker. (K1D, K1L) to end of round. **Palm. Left Hand.** (K1L, K1D) until 3 stitches remain in round. Place marker. Make 1 Right with L. K1L. Make 1 Left with L. Place marker. K1D, K1L.

There will be 3 L stitches between markers. This sets up 24 Spring Ice stitches on the front of the mitten and S&P stitches on the palm, with the thumb gusset stitches inside the markers.

Round 2. Front. Work Round 2 of the Spring Ice chart 3 times. **Palm.** Work S&P to marker. Slip marker. Work Round

2 of thumb gusset chart to next marker. Slip marker. Work S&P to end of round.

Continue in patterns as established, working successive rounds of the thumb gusset chart between markers until Round 14 is complete.

Next Round. Front. Work Round 1 of the Spring Ice chart on the front. **Palm.** Work S&P to marker, remove marker. Place gusset stitches on a holder. Cast on 1 stitch with L to bridge the gap. Remove marker. S&P to end of round (47 stitches).

Continue working successive rounds of Spring Ice on the front of the mitten and S&P on the palm, until a total of 25 rounds are complete, ending with Spring Ice Round 11. **Left Hand Only.** Break yarns.

Reserve Trigger Finger Stitches. Use lengths of waste yarn for stitch holders. With Spring Ice facing, and beginning at the same edge of the mitten as the thumb gusset, place 8 stitches of the front and the corresponding 8 S&P stitches of the palm on holders for trigger finger (31 stitches).

Right Hand. With Spring Ice facing, and beginning with K1D, work 15 front stitches in S&P. Cast on 2 stitches in correct S&P order to bridge the gap. Work palm in S&P (33 stitches).

Photo: J. Leaning

Left Hand. With palm facing, rejoin yarns at the edge of the mitten opposite the thumb and work stitches of the palm in S&P. Cast on 2 stitches in correct S&P order to bridge the gap. Work front in S&P, maintaining continuity (33 stitches).

Both Hands. Work 12 rounds more in S&P or until work reaches tip of little finger, ending with Spring Ice facing for next round.

Shape Top. Arrange stitches 16, 9, 8. Note that Shaping Round 1 produces adjacent stitches of the same colour at 4 points in the round. These are eliminated on the following round. **Shaping Round 1. Front.** K1 with correct S&P colour. SSK with next colour in the sequence. Work S&P until 3 stitches remain on front needle. K2tog with the same colour as the stitch just made. K1 in correct colour of S&P. **Palm.** Work as for front (4 stitches decreased).

Shaping Round 2. Front. K1 in S&P. SSK with next colour in the sequence. S&P to last 3 stitches of front. K2tog with next colour as the stitch just made. K1 in S&P. **Palm.** Work as for front (4 stitches decreased.)

Shaping Round 3. Work in S&P without decreasing.

Repeat shaping Rounds 1–3 once (17 stitches). Break L, leaving a 3-inch tail. Break D, leaving a 12-inch tail. The hand is finished with a 3-needle bind off on the wrong side of the work.

3-Needle Bind Off. Place stitches of front on a length of waste yarn. Place stitches of palm on another length of yarn. Turn mitten inside out to work bind off on the wrong side, using the long tail of D. Return stitches on holders to 2 thinner double-pointed needles for easier working. Hold these needles parallel to one another, with the needle with the greater number of stitches nearest you. With a third double-pointed needle and D, K1 from the needle nearest you. Then knit 1 stitch from the front needle nearest you together with 1 stitch of the opposite colour from the back needle. 2 stitches now on the working needle. Pass first stitch on working needle over second stitch to cast it off. 1 stitch remains on working needle. Continue to knit together 1 stitch from front and back holding needles and slipping the first stitch over the second stitch on the working needle to cast off. Repeat until 1 stitch remains. Fasten off and darn ends.

Trigger Finger. Transfer 8 stitches from front holder to a double-pointed needle. Place 8 stitches from palm on a double-pointed needle.

Right Trigger Finger. With Spring Ice facing, rejoin yarns and work Spring Ice Round 12 on 8 stitches of front. Work

To make a hand: *to have success. I can remember several times I tried to spin some wool on the old spinning wheel, but I never could make any hand at it.*

—DICTIONARY OF NEWFOUNDLAND ENGLISH

S&P on 8 stitches of palm. With another double-pointed needle, pick up and knit 3 stitches in correct S&P sequence from the base of the hand (19 stitches).

Left Trigger Finger. With Spring Ice facing, rejoin yarns and work Spring Ice Round 12 on 8 stitches of front. Pick up and knit 3 stitches in correct S&P sequence (K1D, K1L, K1D) from the hand. Work S&P on 8 stitches of the palm (19 stitches).

Work successive rounds of Spring Ice on the first 8 stitches of trigger finger and S&P on the remaining 11 stitches until Round 11 of Spring Ice is complete. Work 1 round of S&P on all 19 stitches, or continue S&P until the work reaches the tip of the index finger.

Finger Decrease Round 1. (K1 with correct colour in S&P sequence. K2tog with next colour in sequence. K1 in S&P). Repeat to end of round, working leftover stitches in S&P (15 stitches). Adjacent stitches in the same colour will be eliminated in the next round.

Finger Decrease Round 2. (K1 with correct S&P colour, K2tog with next colour in S&P sequence), working 3 leftover stitches in S&P (11 stitches). Break yarns. Thread through remaining stitches and secure.

Thumb. Transfer thumb stitches from holder to 2 double-pointed needles. Rejoin yarns and knit these stitches in S&P. With another needle, pick up and knit 4 stitches in S&P at the base of the thumb (19 stitches). Work 12 rounds in S&P. Decrease as for fingers.

Finishing. Darn ends securely. Press lightly, omitting ribbing.

© Shirley A. Scott 2018

HANGASHORE
Trigger Mitts for Men

DEGREE OF DIFFICULTY: ✳ ✳ TANGLY

In days gone by a man who was regarded as too lazy to fish was known as a hangashore. The term eventually came to embrace a wide range of rascals, including mischievous children. The *Dictionary of Newfoundland English* records that a hangashore was "too bad to be called a good-for-nothin' but not bad enough to be called a sleeveen." The bold graphic appearance of this mitten makes us think of certain lighthouses scattered around our shores.

MATERIALS

Two shades of Briggs and Little Regal 2-ply worsted weight wool, 1 skein in Dark (D), 1 skein in Light (L). 1 set of 4.00 mm double-pointed needles. 2 thinner double-pointed needles for 3-needle bind off only (optional). Ring markers.

SIZE

Men's Medium. Circumference: 8.5 inches (22.5 cm). Length of mitten from beginning of Hangashore pattern: 7.5 inches (18 cm). Trigger finger: 2.5 inches (6.5 cm). Thumb: 3 inches (8 cm). Length of hand, thumb, and trigger finger is adjustable.

GAUGE

24 stitches x 28 rows = 4 inches (10 cm).

SALT AND PEPPER PATTERN (S&P)

Worked over an odd number of stitches.
Round 1. (K1D, K1L). Repeat to end of round.
Round 2. (K1L, K1D). Repeat to end of round.

Knit: *The activity of making or repairing a fish net.*

—DICTIONARY OF NEWFOUNDLAND ENGLISH

Bonavista lighthouse.

HANGASHORE CHART (27 stitches x 8 rows)

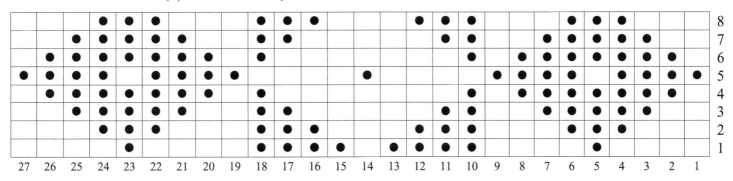

HANGASHORE THUMB GUSSET CHART

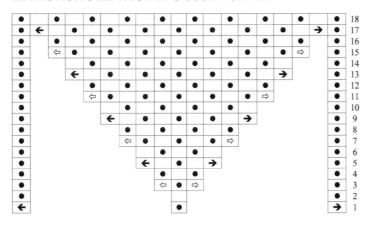

- ● K1D
- → Make 1 Right with D
- ⇦ Make 1 Left with L

Empty square = K1L
- ← Make 1 Left with D
- ⇨ Make 1 Right with L

Work charts from right to left, bottom to top. Always carry D on the left and L on the right to prevent streaks in the work.

Instructions are for both hands unless otherwise indicated.

Wrist. With D cast on 42 stitches. Join in a circle, being careful not to twist. Work 27 rounds (K2, P1) ribbing in a striped pattern of your choice. **Next Round.** With D knit, increasing 12 stitches evenly spaced (54 stitches). Arrange 27 stitches on needle 1 for the front of the mitten. Divide remaining stitches on needles 2 and 3 for the palm.

Round 1. Front. Always carrying D ahead (i.e., on the left), join L and work Round 1 of the Hangashore chart for the front of the mitten (27 stitches). **Palm. Right Hand.** K1D, K1L. Place marker. Make 1 right-leaning increase (M1R) with D. K1D. Make 1 left-leaning increase (M1L) with D. Place marker. (K1L, K1D) to end of round. There will be 3 D stitches between markers. **Palm. Left Hand.** (K1D, K1L)

until 3 stitches remain in round. Place marker. M1R with D. K1D. M1L with D. Place marker. K1L. K1D. There will be 3 D stitches between markers.

This sets up 27 Hangashore stitches on the front of the mitten and S&P stitches on the palm, with the thumb gusset stitches between markers. The gusset is outlined with D stitches inside the markers.

Round 2. Front. Work Round 2 of the Hangashore chart. **Palm.** Work S&P to marker. Slip marker. Work Round 2 of thumb gusset chart to next marker. Slip marker. Work S&P to end of round.

Continue in Hangashore pattern on front and S&P on palm as established, working successive rows of thumb gusset chart between markers until Round 8 of Hangashore and thumb gusset is complete. **Next Round.** Work Round 1 of Hangashore pattern on front. **Palm.** Work in S&P to marker. Work Round 9 of thumb gusset pattern between markers. Work S&P to end of round. **Next Round.** Work Round 2 of Hangashore pattern on front. **Palm.** Work S&P to marker. Work Round 10 of thumb gusset chart between markers. Work S&P to end of round.

Continue working Hangashore on the front and thumb gusset chart between markers on the palm until Round 18 of thumb gusset is complete. There will be 19 gusset stitches between markers.

Next Round. Front. Work next round of Hangashore on the front. **Palm.** S&P to marker. Remove marker. Place gusset stitches on a holder. Cast on 1 stitch with D to bridge the gap. Remove marker. S&P to end of round (54 stitches).

Continue working Hangashore on the front of the mitten and S&P on the palm until a total of 25 pattern rounds are complete, ending with Hangashore Round 1. Work S&P on the palm.

Next Round. Beginning with K1L, work S&P on 27 front stitches. Make 1 with D. Work in S&P on palm (55 stitches). Work 2 rounds more in continuous S&P.

Reserve Trigger Finger Stitches. Use lengths of waste yarn for stitch holders. **Right Hand.** With front facing, work 20 stitches in S&P. Place next 8 stitches of front on holder for trigger finger. Place corresponding 7 stitches of palm on holder for trigger finger. Cast on 3 stitches in correct S&P order to bridge the gap. Work S&P to end of round (43 stitches).

Left Hand. Break yarns. Place first 8 stitches of front on holder for trigger finger. Place the corresponding 7 stitches of palm on holder for trigger finger. With Hangashore facing, rejoin yarns and work S&P on front. Work S&P on palm. Cast on 3 stitches in S&P to bridge gap (43 stitches).

HORIZONS

The island of Newfoundland has 9,656 kilometres of coastline. People who live in this rocky place spend hours gazing at the horizon, a magnet one cannot turn away from. The experience can be liminal. Does it awaken a latent sense of adventure at sea that yearns to be satisfied? Has the human soul always craved knowing what is beyond the vanishing point?

For centuries Newfoundlanders have scanned the horizon watching for ships that brought supplies, loved ones, medical services, the Good News, and more. We watch the sunrise and the sunset. We watch an approaching gale. We watch for a break in the fog and then gaze in wonder at the clear blue sky and sea. We watch for the spring ice and then the mighty icebergs.

We are always watching and waiting.

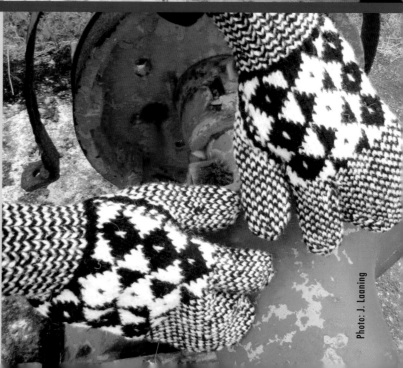

Both Hands. Work 13 rounds more in S&P, ending with Hangashore facing for next round. Arrange stitches 21, 11, 11.

Shape Top. Note that some shaping rounds produce 2 adjacent stitches in the same colour at 4 points in the round. These will be eliminated in the following round.

Shaping Round 1. Front. K1 with correct S&P colour. SSK with next colour in the sequence. Work S&P until 3 stitches remain on front needle. K2tog with the same colour as the stitch just made. K1 in correct colour of S&P. **Palm.** Work as for front (4 stitches decreased).

Shaping Round 2. Front. K1 in S&P. SSK with next colour in the sequence. S&P to last 3 stitches of front. K2tog with next colour in the sequence. K1 in S&P. **Palm.** Work as front (4 stitches decreased).

Shaping Round 3. Work in S&P without decreasing.
Repeat shaping Rounds 1–3 twice (19 stitches). Break L,

leaving a 3-inch tail. Break D, leaving a 14-inch tail.

3-Needle Bind Off. The hand is finished with a 3-needle bind off on the wrong side of the work.

Place stitches of front on a length of waste yarn. Place stitches of palm on another length of yarn. Turn mitten inside out to work bind off on the wrong side, using the long tail of D.

Return stitches on holders to 2 thinner double-pointed needles for easier working. Hold these needles parallel to one another, the needle with the greater number of stitches nearest you. With a third double-pointed needle and D, K1 from the holding needle nearest you. Then knit 1 stitch from the front needle together with 1 stitch of the opposite colour from the back needle. There are now 2 stitches on the working needle. Pass first stitch on working needle over second stitch to cast it off. 1 stitch remains on working needle. Continue to knit together 1 stitch from front and back needles and slipping the first stitch over second stitch on the working needle to cast off. Repeat until 1 stitch remains. Fasten off.

Trigger Finger. Transfer 8 stitches from front holder to a double-pointed needle. Place 7 stitches from palm on a double-pointed needle.

Right Trigger Finger. With Hangashore facing, rejoin yarns and work stitches on front and palm in S&P. With another double-pointed needle, pick up and knit 6 stitches in correct S&P sequence from the base of the hand (21 stitches).

Left Trigger Finger. With Hangashore facing, rejoin yarns and work 8 stitches of front in S&P. Pick up and knit 6 stitches in correct colour sequence from base of hand. Work 7 palm stitches in S&P (21 stitches).

Both Hands. Note beginning of round. Divide stitches on 3 double-pointed needles and work 16 more rounds of S&P, or until work reaches the tip of the index finger.

Finger Decrease Round 1. (K1 with correct colour in S&P sequence. K2tog with next colour in sequence. K1 in S&P). Repeat to end of round, working any leftover stitches in S&P. Adjacent stitches in the same colour will be eliminated in the next round.

Finger Decrease Round 2. (K1 with correct S&P colour. K2tog with next colour in S&P sequence). Repeat to end of round, working any leftover stitches in S&P. Break yarns. Thread through remaining stitches and secure.

Thumb. Transfer thumb stitches from holder to 2 double-pointed needles. Rejoin yarns and knit these stitches in S&P. With another needle, pick up and knit 2 stitches in S&P at the base of the thumb (21 stitches). Note beginning of round. Work 15 rounds more in S&P. Decrease as for fingers.

Finishing. Darn ends securely. Press lightly under a damp cloth, omitting ribbing.

© Shirley A. Scott 2018

BIG DIAMONDS

Forever and Solitaire—Two Classic Mitten Designs for Young Maids

DEGREE OF DIFFICULTY: * EASY DOES IT

Diamond motifs are seen everywhere in Newfoundland, but especially in traditional mittens. They are quite easy to knit, yet they produce dramatic results. Patterns often contain more than one type. These motifs are called by many names—big diamonds, half diamonds, quarter diamonds, plus Labrador diamonds and St. Mary's Bay diamonds in many versions. This identifies but a few of our marvellous, distinctive diamond mitten patterns. Here are two new ones to add to the repertoire.

Big Diamonds is a single pattern with two interchangeable variations, Forever and Solitaire. Our adventurous take on diamond patterns is inspired by a mitten seen years ago and by all the architectural diamond shapes seen on buildings in Newfoundland from past to present. Like engagement rings, these toasty mittens are symbols of love.

SIZE

To fit a young lady's hand. Circumference: 8.25 inches (21.5 cm). Length from beginning of diamond motif to the cast off: 7.25 inches (18.25 cm).

MATERIALS

Briggs and Little Heritage worsted weight wool, 1 skein Dark (D), 1 skein Light (L). 1 set 3.75 mm double-pointed needles. Ring markers, darning needle, stitch holders.

GAUGE

12 stitches x 11 rounds = 2 inches (5 cm) in S&P pattern.

Look at those young maidens out beatin' the path! This meant walking along Church Street, Bonavista after supper and before dark, in hopes of courting.

—HAROLD THOMPSON (1900-1992), BONAVISTA

FOREVER CHART

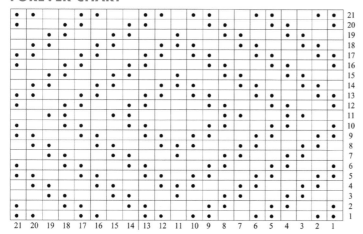

- K1D   Empty square = K1L

SOLITAIRE CHART

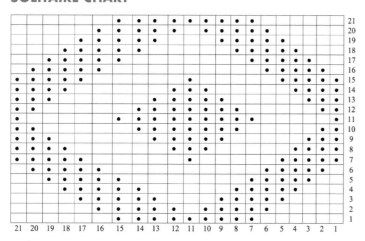

BIG DIAMONDS THUMB GUSSET CHART

- K1D   Empty square = K1L
- ⇐ Make 1 Left with L   ⇨ Make 1 Right with L

SALT AND PEPPER PATTERN (S&P)

Worked on an odd number of stitches.

Round 1. (K1D, K1L). Repeat to end of round.

Round 2. (K1L, K1D). Repeat to end of round.

Work charts from right to left, bottom to top. Always carry D on the left and L on the right to prevent streaks in the work. This mitten features a choice of stitch patterns. Both variations are 21 stitches x 21 rounds and are interchangeable. Instructions are for both hands unless otherwise noted. The thumb gusset is outlined in a D stitch. Weave in the colour not in use when it is carried for more than 3 stitches. Please read all instructions before casting on.

Wrist. With D, cast on 36 stitches. Join in a round, being careful not to twist. Work 19 rounds of (K2, P1) ribbing in a solid colour or a stripe of your choice. **Round 20.** Work in ribbing, increasing 8 stitches evenly spaced (44 stitches).

Right Hand. Arrange stitches on needles as follows. Needle 1: 21 stitches (front of mitten). Needle 2: 12 stitches. Needle 3: 11 stitches. **Round 1.** Join L. Needle 1. Work Round 1 of the chosen chart for front of mitten. Needle 2. Place marker. Work Round 1 (increase round) of the thumb gusset chart. Place marker. Work Round 1 of S&P on remaining stitches of needle 2. On needle 3, continue Round 1 of S&P to end of round for the palm of the mitten. **Round 2.** Work Round 2 of Diamond chart. Slip marker. Work Round 2 of thumb gusset chart. Slip marker. Work Round 2 of S&P to end of round. Continue in this established manner until Round 15 is complete. **Round 16.** Work Round 16 of Diamond chart. Slip marker. Place the 13 thumb gusset stitches on a holder. Cast on 4 stitches in the correct colour sequence to bridge the gap. Work S&P to the end of the round (45 stitches). Thumb gusset is now complete.

Continue to work rounds of Diamond chart on the front and S&P on the palm until chart is complete. Finish the round in S&P. Work 8 rounds more in S&P on all stitches,

MAID
A woman; a young unmarried girl or daughter.

MAID RACKET
Courting.
An' we'd go down practically every night on the maid racket.

—*DICTIONARY OF NEWFOUNDLAND ENGLISH*

or desired length, ending with Round 2 of S&P. Slip 1 stitch from beginning of needle 2 to the end of needle 1. Needle 1: 22 stitches. The 23 stitches for the palm are shared between needle 2 and needle 3. Proceed to Shape Top.

Left Hand. Arrange stitches as follows. Needle 1: 21 stitches (front of the mitten). Needle 2: 11 stitches. Needle 3: 12 stitches. **Round 1.** Join L. Work Round 1 of chosen Diamond chart on needle 1. Work Round 1 of S&P on needle 2. Continue S&P on needle 3 until 3 stitches remain on needle. Place marker. Work Round 1 (increase round) of thumb gusset chart. Place marker. **Round 2.** Work Round 2 of Diamond chart. Work S&P to marker. Slip marker. Work Round 2 of the thumb gusset chart. Slip marker. Continue established pattern until Round 15 is complete. **Round 16.** Work Round 16 of Diamond chart. Work S&P pattern to marker. Remove marker. Slip 13 thumb gusset stitches to a holder. Cast on 4 stitches in correct colour sequence to bridge the gap (45 stitches). Thumb gusset is now complete.

Continue working Diamond chart on the front and S&P on the palm until Round 21 is complete. Work 7 rounds more, or desired length, in S&P on all stitches, ending with Round 2 of S&P. **Next Round.** Work S&P until 1 stitch remains in the round. Slip this stitch to the beginning of needle 1 (22 stitches). 23 palm stitches are divided between needle 2 and needle 3. Proceed to Shape Top.

Photo courtesy J. Pratt

ADVICE TO THE YOUNG

I enjoys knitting. It's a lot better for yous to be in your rooms sitting down and doing a bit of knitting ... rather than be out beatin' around. 'Cause if you was out beatin' around you only gets a bad name.

—ELIZABETH WARNER "KNITTING A GLOVE: ONE ASPECT OF ONE WOMAN'S KNITTING"

Shape Top. Decreases are made 1 stitch from the end of the needles at 4 points in the round. 2 decrease rounds are followed by a round with no decreases.

Shaping Round 1. Needle 1. K1 in correct colour. SSK with the next colour in the sequence. Resume pattern on next stitch (having made 2 stitches of same colour). Work in pattern until 3 stitches remain before the end of the needle. K2tog in the same colour as the stitch just made. Work last stitch in correct colour. Needle 2. K1, SSK as above. Work in pattern to end of needle. On needle 3, work in pattern until 3 stitches remain in round. K2tog in the same colour as the stitch just made. K1 in correct colour. **Shaping Round 2.** Work SSK and K2tog decreases at the same points as the previous round. Correct colour sequence will be restored. **Shaping Round 3.** Work in S&P without decreasing. Repeat these 3 rounds until 21 stitches remain, ending after Shaping Round 3 is complete. Cast off using 3-needle bind off.

3-Needle Bind Off. Place the stitches from the front of the mitten on a length of waste yarn. Place the stitches of the palm on another length of yarn. Turn the mitten inside out to work the bind off on the wrong side. Return the stitches from the holders to 2 thinner double-pointed needles for convenience. Hold these needles parallel to one another. Have the needle with the greater number of stitches nearest you. With a third

needle, and using the long tail of D, K1 from the holding needle nearest you. Then knit 1 stitch from the front needle together with 1 stitch of the opposite colour from the back needle. You now have 2 stitches on the working needle. Pass first stitch on the working needle over the second stitch to cast it off. 1 stitch remains on the working needle. Continue to knit together 1 stitch from the front and back holding needles and slipping the first stitch over the second stitch on the working needle to cast off. Repeat until 1 stitch remains. Fasten off and darn in ends.

Thumb. Slip 13 gusset stitches from holder to 2 needles. Rejoin yarns and knit these stitches in correct S&P sequence. With a third needle, pick up and knit 6 stitches in S&P at the base of the mitten (19 stitches). Work 11 rounds more or desired length in S&P. **Thumb Decrease Round 1.** (Knit first stitch in correct colour sequence. K2tog with next colour. K1 with the same colour as the stitch just worked). Repeat to end of round, knitting any remaining stitches in S&P. **Thumb Decrease Round 2.** (K1, K2tog) in S&P to the end of the round, working any remaining stitches in S&P. Break yarns, draw up and fasten securely.

Finishing. Carefully darn in all ends and trim neatly. Press under a damp cloth, omitting ribbing.

© Christine LeGrow 2018

MUMMERS
Classic Mitts for Ladies

DEGREE OF DIFFICULTY: ∗ EASY DOES IT

Mummering, or jannying as it is also known, is a venerable Newfoundland tradition, filling with merriment the cold, dark nights between Boxing Day and Old Christmas Day. In its original form, this ancient custom saw wandering bands of heavily disguised mummers paying impromptu and unbidden visits to homes in the community, begging food and drink in exchange for music and dance. Guessing the identity of the mummers was the object of the game. Mummering has recently regained popularity and many communities now sponsor mummers' parades. This colourful mitten features a snug fit, a smoothly rounded top, and a thumb gusset outlined in Light stitches.

MATERIALS

2 shades of Briggs and Little Regal 2-ply worsted weight wool, 1 skein in Dark (D), 1 skein in Light (L). 1 set of 4.00 mm double-pointed needles. Two thinner double-pointed needles for 3-needle bind off only (optional). Ring markers or yarn markers.

SIZE

Ladies' Medium. Circumference: 7.5 inches (18 cm). Length of mitten from beginning of Mummers pattern: 7 inches (18 cm). Thumb: 2.5 inches (6 cm). Length is adjustable.

GAUGE

24 stitches x 28 rows = 4 inches (10 cm).

SALT AND PEPPER PATTERN (S&P)

Worked over an odd number of stitches.

Round 1. (K1D, K1L). Repeat to end of round.

Round 2. (K1L, K1D). Repeat to end of round.

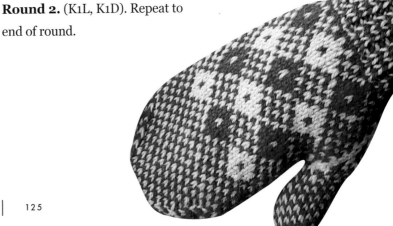

MUMMERS CHART (25 stitches x 14 rows)

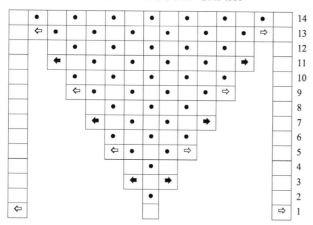

MUMMERS THUMB GUSSET CHART

- ● K1D
- → Make 1 Right with D
- ⇦ Make 1 Left with L

Empty square = K1L
- ⇐ Make 1 Left with D
- ⇨ Make 1 Right with L

Work charts from right to left, bottom to top. Always carry D on the left and L on the right to prevent streaks in the work. Instructions are for both hands unless otherwise indicated.

Wrist. With L, or the colour of your choice, cast on 36 stitches. Join in a circle, being careful not to twist. Work 27 rounds in (K2, P1) ribbing in a striped pattern. **Next Round.** Knit, increasing 13 stitches evenly spaced (49 stitches). Arrange 25 stitches on needle 1 for the front of the mitten. Divide remaining 24 stitches on needles 2 and 3 for palm.

Round 1. Front. Always carrying D ahead, work Round 1 of Mummers chart for the front of the mitten (25 stitches).

Photo: S.N. LeGrow

66 There's big ones 'n small ones 'n
tall ones 'n thin
Boys dressed as women and
girls dressed as men.
Humps on their backs an' mitts
on their feet
My blessed, we'll die with the heat. 99

– "THE MUMMERS SONG," SIMANI

Palm. Right Hand. K1D, K1L, K1D. Place marker. Make 1 right-leaning increase with Light (M1R with L). K1L. Make 1 left-leaning increase with L (M1L with L). Place marker. (K1D, K1L) to end of round. There will be 3 L stitches between markers. **Palm. Left Hand.** (K1D, K1L) until 3 stitches remain in round. Place marker. M1R with L. K1L. M1L with L. Place marker. K1D, K1L. There will be 3 L stitches between markers.

This sets up 25 Mummers pattern stitches on the front of the mitten and S&P stitches on the palm, with the thumb gusset stitches between markers. The gusset is outlined with L stitches inside the markers.

Round 2. Front. Work Round 2 of the Mummers chart. **Palm.** Work S&P to marker. Slip marker. Work Round 2 of thumb gusset chart to next marker. Slip marker. Work S&P to end of round.

Continue in Mummers pattern on front and S&P on palm as established, working successive rows of thumb gusset chart between markers until Round 14 of Mummers and thumb gusset charts is complete. There will be 15 gusset stitches between markers.

Next Round. Front. Work Round 1 of Mummers pattern. **Palm.** Work S&P to marker. Remove marker. Place gusset stitches on a holder. Cast on 1 stitch with L to bridge the gap. Remove marker. S&P to end of round (48 stitches).

Continue working Mummers pattern on the front of the mitten and S&P on the palm until 28 Mummers pattern rounds (2 vertical repeats of the Mummers chart) are complete. S&P on palm.

Next Round. Beginning with K1L, work S&P on front stitches. Work S&P on palm (49 stitches). Arrange stitches 24, 13, 12.

Work 7 rounds more in continuous S&P, ending with Mummers facing for next round.

Shape Top. Note that some shaping rounds produce 2 adjacent stitches in the same colour at 4 points in the round, positioned as on the toe of a sock. These will be eliminated in the following round.

Shaping Round 1. Front. K1 with correct S&P colour. SSK with next colour in the sequence. Work S&P until 3 stitches remain on front needle. K2tog with the same colour as the stitch just made. K1 in correct colour of S&P. **Palm.** Work as for front (4 stitches decreased).

Shaping Round 2. Front. K1 in S&P. SSK with next colour in the sequence. S&P to last 3 stitches of front. K2tog with next colour in the sequence. K1 in S&P. **Palm.** Work as for front (4 stitches decreased).

Shaping Round 3. Work in S&P without decreasing.

Repeat Shaping Rounds 1–3 two more times (25 stitches). Break L, leaving a 3-inch tail. Break D, leaving a 14-inch tail.

3-Needle Bind Off. Place stitches of front on a length of waste yarn. Place stitches of palm on another length of yarn. Turn mitten inside out to work bind off on the wrong side, using the long tail of D.

Return stitches on holders to 2 thinner double-pointed needles for easier working. Hold these needles parallel to one another, the needle with the greater number of stitches nearest you. With a third double-pointed needle and D, K1 from the holding needle nearest you. Then knit 1 stitch from the front needle together with 1 stitch of the opposite colour from the back needle. You now have 2 stitches on the working needle. Pass first stitch on working needle over second stitch to cast it off. 1 stitch remains on working needle. Continue to knit together 1 stitch from front and back needles and slipping the first stitch over the second stitch on the working needle to cast off. Repeat until 1 stitch remains. Fasten off and darn ends.

Thumb. Transfer thumb stitches from holder to 2 double-pointed needles. Rejoin yarns and knit these stitches in S&P. With another needle, pick up and knit 4 stitches in S&P at the base of the thumb (19 stitches). Note beginning of round. Work 12 rounds more in S&P, or to desired length.

Thumb Decrease Round 1. (K1 with correct colour in S&P sequence. K2tog with next colour in sequence. K1 in S&P). Repeat to end of round, working any leftover stitches in S&P. Adjacent stitches in the same colour will be eliminated in the next round.

Thumb Decrease Round 2. (K1 with correct S&P colour, K2tog with next colour in S&P sequence). Repeat to end of round, working any leftover stitches in S&P. Break yarns. Thread through remaining stitches and secure.

Finishing. Darn ends securely. Press lightly, omitting ribbing.

© Shirley A. Scott 2018

SIGNAL HILL
Classic Mittens for Ladies

DEGREE OF DIFFICULTY: * EASY DOES IT

Do you see the dots and dashes in this design? On Signal Hill on December 12, 1901, Guglielmo Marconi received the first ever transatlantic wireless signal, sent in Morse code from Poldhu, Cornwall. Global communication was never the same again.

We first saw this stitch pattern in a pair of socks worn over the muddy shoes of a mummer in St. John's annual Mummers Parade. We adapted it to our mittens. Close study suggests that it may have begun life as a happy mistake made in a conventional pattern where dark and light diamonds alternated within each tier. What an appealing mistake it is, full of artistic possibilities. The Signal Hill Mitten lends itself to daring colour combinations.

MATERIALS

1 skein Briggs and Little Regal 2-ply worsted weight wool in Dark (D). 1 or more skeins of Regal in Light (L). If using more than 1 contrast colour (L), oddments are sufficient. 1 set of 4.00 mm double-pointed needles. Ring markers.

SIZE

Ladies' Medium. Circumference: 8 inches (20 cm). Length from cast on to tip: 11 inches (28 cm). Length is adjustable. Change gauge to change size.

GAUGE

22 stitches x 24 rows = 4 inches (10 cm).

SIGNAL HILL CHART (14 rows x 25 stitches)

	25	8	7	6	5	4	3	2	1
14	●	●	●	●		●	●	●	●
13	●	●	●				●	●	●
12	●	●						●	●
11					●				
10							●	●	●
9						●	●	●	●
8	●	●	●	●		●	●	●	●
7					●				
6				●	●	●			
5			●	●	●	●	●		
4	●	●		●		●	●	●	●
3				●	●	●			
2					●	●			
1					●				

SIGNAL HILL THUMB GUSSET CHART

(14 rows, chart worked with increases forming a gusset triangle. Symbols: ● = K1D, empty = K1L, ← Make 1 Left with D, → Make 1 Right with D, ⇐ Make 1 Left with L, ⇒ Make 1 Right with L)

Photo: J. Laaning

Legend:

- ● K1D
- Empty square = K1L
- → Make 1 Right with D
- ← Make 1 Left with D
- ⇐ Make 1 Left with L
- ⇒ Make 1 Right with L

SALT AND PEPPER PATTERN (S&P)

Worked over an odd number of stitches.

Round 1. (K1D, K1L). Repeat to end of round.

Round 2. (K1L, K1D). Repeat to end of round.

Work charts from right to left, bottom to top. Always carry D on the left and L on the right to prevent streaks in the work. Instructions are for both hands unless otherwise stated.

Wrist. With D, or the colour of your choice, cast on 36 stitches and join in a round, being careful not to twist. Work 27 rounds of (K2, P1) ribbing in a striped pattern of your choice.

Increase for Hand. With D, knit 1 round, increasing 12 stitches evenly spaced (48 stitches). Place 25 stitches on the first needle for the front of the mitten. Divide the remaining stitches conveniently on 2 needles for palm. The front will be worked in Signal Hill pattern and the palm in S&P.

On each round of the Signal Hill chart, work stitches 1–8 three times, then stitch 25 once. Introduce a new contrasting Light colour on Rounds 8–14 if desired. Weave unused colour in at regular intervals.

Round 1. Front. Work stitches 1–8 of Round 1 of Signal Hill chart 3 times on front. Work stitch 25 once. **Palm. Right Hand.** Knit 1 with Dark (K1D). Knit 1 with Light (K1L). Place

marker. Make 1 right (M1R) with D, to create the right-leaning outline stitch. K1D to establish the point of the thumb gusset. Make 1 left (M1L) with D to create the left-leaning outline stitch. Place marker. There will be 3 adjacent D stitches. Beginning with K1L, work in S&P to end of round. **Palm. Left Hand.** (K1D, K1L) until 3 stitches remain in round. Place marker. M1R with D to create the right-leaning outline stitch. K1D to establish the point of the thumb gusset. M1L with D to create the left-leaning outline stitch. Place marker. There will be 3 adjacent D stitches. K1L, K1D.

Round 2. Front. Work stitches 1–8 of Round 2 of Signal Hill pattern 3 times on the front. Work stitch 25 once. **Palm.** Work in S&P to marker. Slip marker. Work Round 2 of the thumb gusset chart between the markers as follows: K1D outline stitch. K1L gusset stitch. K1D outline stitch. Slip marker. Work in S&P to end of round.

Round 3. Front. Work stitches 1–8 of Round 3 of Signal Hill pattern 3 times on the front. Work stitch 25 once. **Palm.**

Work in S&P to marker. Slip marker. Work Round 3 of thumb gusset chart to next marker. Slip marker. S&P to end of round.

Continue working successive rounds of Signal Hill on the front of the mitten and the palm in S&P with the thumb gusset chart inside the markers, until the thumb gusset chart has been completed. There are now 15 gusset stitches inside the markers. Finish round in S&P.

Next Round. Work Signal Hill pattern on the front. Work S&P on palm to marker. Remove marker. Put next 15 thumb gusset stitches on a holder. Remove marker. Cast on 1 stitch with D to bridge the gap. Work S&P to end of round. Thumb gusset is now complete.

Next Round. Work Signal Hill pattern on the front, S&P on the palm. Continue in pattern until 28 rounds of Signal Hill pattern are complete on the front. Work S&P on palm to end of round.

Next Round. Beginning with K1D, work 25 stitches of front in S&P. Cast on 1 stitch with L. Work S&P on palm (49 stitches).

Photo: J. Laaning

Work 8 rounds more in continuous S&P, ending with Signal Hill facing for next round.

Shape Picket Fence Top. Decreases are made 1 stitch in from the edge at 4 points in the round, positioned as on the toe of a sock. Decreases are made on every round.

Shaping Round 1. Front. K1 in correct colour. SSK with the next colour in the sequence. Resume S&P pattern on next stitch, having made 2 adjacent stitches of the same colour. Work in pattern until 3 stitches remain on front. K2tog in the same colour as the stitch just made. Work last stitch in correct colour. **Palm.** As front.

Shaping Round 2. Front. K1. SSK in next colour. Work in S&P until 3 stitches remain on front. K2tog in same colour as the stitch just made, K1. **Palm.** As front. Correct colour sequence is restored.

Repeat these 2 shaping rounds until 11 stitches remain. Break yarns. Thread D into a darning needle and pass through remaining stitches. Tighten and secure. Proceed to Thumb.

Thumb. Transfer thumb gusset stitches to 2 needles (8, 7 stitches). Join yarns and work thumb stitches in S&P. Pick up and knit 4 stitches at the base of the thumb in correct S&P order (19 stitches). Note beginning of round. Work 12 rounds more in S&P or until work reaches the tip of the thumb.

Decrease Round 1. (K1 with correct S&P colour. K2tog with next colour in sequence. K1 in S&P). Repeat to end of round, knitting last 3 stitches in S&P (15 stitches).

Decrease Round 2. (K1, K2tog) in S&P to end of round, working last 3 stitches in S&P (12 stitches). Break yarns, thread through remaining stitches and secure.

Finishing. Darn ends securely. Press mitten well under a damp cloth. Do not press ribbing.

© Shirley A. Scott 2018

Signal Hill Mitten.

ST. MARY'S BAY
Trigger Mitts for Youngsters

DEGREE OF DIFFICULTY: * EASY DOES IT

St Mary's Bay (N46°50'00", W53°45'54") is impressive in its beauty. It is bordered to the east by Trepassey Bay, sometimes called the foggiest place on earth, and to the west by Placentia Bay, Newfoundland's largest bay. For hundreds of years the cod fishery has sustained the inhabitants of the tiny communities that dot its coast. The moratorium on cod fishing in 1992 was a turning point in the history of Newfoundland. Since then our fishery has diversified.

Cape St. Mary's Ecological Reserve with its huge nesting gannet colony and numerous other species of birds is a birder's paradise. Beaches at Point La Haye and St. Vincent's are superb natural scenic attractions. St. Mary's Bay Trigger Mitts for Youngsters were inspired by the many diamond patterns knit into mittens there for many generations. The colours chosen in this pair reflect the colours found at the Cape St. Mary's Ecological Reserve.

SIZE

Youngsters' Medium. Circumference: 8.25 inches (21.5 cm).

Length measured from beginning of the St. Mary's Bay motif to cast off: 6 inches (15 cm).

MATERIALS

Briggs and Little Regal 2-ply worsted weight wool. Oddments in 2 Light (L) colours and 2 Dark (D) colours. 1 set size 3.25 mm double-pointed needles. Ring markers, darning needle, stitch holders.

GAUGE

13 stitches x 12 rows = 2 inches (5 cm) when worked in S&P, using 3.25 mm needles.

SALT AND PEPPER PATTERN (S&P)

Worked on an odd number of stitches.

Round 1. (K1D, K1L). Repeat to end of round.

Round 2. (K1L, K1D). Repeat to end of round.

ST. MARY'S BAY CHART

21	20	19	18	17	16	15	14	13	12	11	10	9	8	7	6	5	4	3	2	1	Row
•	•	•		•	•	•				•				•	•	•		•	•	•	7
•	•			•	•				•		•			•	•				•	•	6
•			•			•		•			•		•			•		•		•	5
		•		•			•					•		•			•		•		4
•		•			•		•				•		•			•				•	3
•	•				•	•			•			•			•	•			•	•	2
•	•	•		•	•	•							•		•	•	•		•	•	1

ST. MARY'S BAY THUMB GUSSET CHART

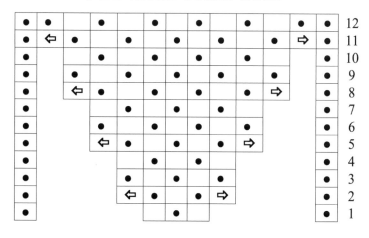

- • K1D
- Empty square = K1L
- ⇦ Make 1 Left with L
- ⇨ Make 1 Right with L

The St. Mary's Bay Trigger Mitt for Youngsters is pictured using four complementary colours. Plan your colour scheme before beginning. The colours are named A-Dark, B-Light, C-Dark, and D-Light.

These colours are used in the following sequence. Pattern Rounds 1–7: A-Dark and B-Light. Rounds 8–14: C-Dark and D-Light. Rounds 15–21: A-Dark and B-Light. 21 rounds complete the diamond pattern.

Break and join yarns at the beginning and end of each 7 round chart repeat.

The thumb, index finger, and top of the mitten are worked in C-Dark and D-Light.

Work charts from right to left, bottom to top. Always carry D on the left and L on the right to prevent colour streaks in your work. All instructions are for both hands unless otherwise indicated. Please read all instructions before casting on.

Wrist. With C-Dark, cast on 40 stitches. Join in round, being careful not to twist. Work (K3, P1) ribbing in your choice of solid colour or stripes until ribbing measures 3 inches (7.5 cm). Increase 7 stitches evenly spaced on final round. Break yarn. Arrange stitches as follows. Needle 1: 21 stitches (front of mitten). Needle 2: 13 stitches. Needle 3: 13 stitches.

Right Hand. Set Up Round. Join and break colours throughout as described above. **Round 1.** Work St. Mary's Bay (SMB) chart. Place marker. Work Round 1 of thumb gusset chart. Place marker. Work Round 1 of S&P to end of round. The SMB chart is now positioned on the front of the mitten, the thumb gusset follows between the markers, and the S&P is established on the palm. **Round 2.** Work Round 2 of SMB chart, Round 2 of thumb gusset chart (increase round), Round 2 of S&P to end of round.

Continue working successive rounds of SMB on the front, thumb gusset, and S&P on the palm until Round 12 is complete. There are 11 thumb gusset stitches between the 2 D outline stitches.

Round 13. Work Round 13 of SMB on the front of the mitten. Remove marker. Slip the 13 stitches of the thumb

gusset, including the 2 D outline stitches, to a holding thread. Cast on 5 stitches in correct colour sequence to bridge the gap. Remove marker. Work S&P to the end of the round. There are 21 stitches on needle 1 (front of mitten). Needles 2 and 3 share the 26 palm stitches. The thumb gusset is now complete. Continue to work SMB chart on the front and S&P on the palm until Round 21 is complete.

Right Index Finger. Slip 2 stitches from the beginning of needle 2 to needle 1 for the front of the mitten (23 stitches on needle 1). Place the last 7 stitches of needle 1 and the first 7 stitches of needle 2 on a holder. These stitches will become part of the first round of the index finger.

Right Hand. Round 22. With SMB facing, join yarns. Keeping S&P colour sequence correct, work S&P on the front of the mitten. Cast on 4 stitches in S&P to bridge the gap. Work S&P to end of round. Work 9 more rounds, or desired length, in S&P.

Set Up Top Shaping. Slip 2 stitches from the beginning of needle 2 to the end of needle 1. Arrange stitches as follows. Needle 1: 18 stitches (front of mitten). Needle 2: 10 stitches. Needle 3: 9 stitches.

Decreasing in S&P Pattern. On odd numbered rounds, decreasing will create 2 adjacent stitches of the same colour. On the following even numbered rounds, these stitches will be worked together, restoring the correct colour sequence.

Shape Top. Decreases are made 1 stitch in from the edge at 4 points in the round. **Shaping Round 1. Needle 1.** K1 in correct colour. SSK with the next colour in the sequence. Resume S&P pattern on the next stitch, having made 2 adjacent stitches of the same colour. Work in pattern until 3 stitches remain on the needle. K2tog in the same colour as the stitch just made. Work the last stitch in correct colour. **Needle 2.** K1, SSK as above, work in pattern to end of the needle. **Needle 3.** Work in pattern until 3 stitches remain before the end of the needle. K2tog in the same colour as the

St. Vincent's Beach.

Point La Haye.

Photo: Shawn Fitzpatrick

stitch just made. K1 in correct colour. **Shaping Round 2.** Work SSK and K2tog decreases in S&P at the same points as the previous round. Colour sequence will be restored. Decrease in this manner until 13 stitches remain. Cast off using 3-needle bind off.

3-Needle Bind Off. Place the stitches from the front of the mitten on a length of waste yarn. Place the stitches of the palm on another length of waste yarn. Turn the mitten inside out to work the bind off. Return the stitches from the threads to 2 thinner double-pointed needles for convenience. Hold these needles parallel to one another. Have the needle with the greater number of stitches nearest you. With a third needle, and using the long tail of D, K1 from the holding needle nearest you. Then knit 1 stitch from the front needle together with 1 stitch of the opposite colour from the back needle. You now have 2 stitches on the working needle. Pass first stitch on the working needle over the second stitch to cast it off. 1 stitch remains on the working needle. Continue to knit together 1 stitch from the front and back needles and slipping the first stitch over the second stitch on the working needle to cast off. Repeat until 1 stitch remains. Thread through remaining stitches. Draw up and fasten securely.

Right Index Finger. With SMB facing, slip first 7 stitches from the holder onto needle 1. Slip next 7 stitches onto a second needle. Join yarns and keeping S&P correct, knit 7 stitches on needle 1, 7 stitches on needle 2. With needle 3, pick up and knit 5 stitches at the base of the finger in the correct colour sequence (19 stitches). Work 13 rounds in S&P, or desired length. Work Finger Decrease Rounds 1 and 2.

Finger Decrease Round 1. (K1 with correct S&P colour. K2tog with next colour in sequence. K1 in S&P). Repeat to end of round, knitting any leftover stitches in S&P. **Finger Decrease Round 2.** (K1, K2tog) in S&P to end of round, working any remaining stitches in S&P. Break yarns, thread though remaining stitches, draw up and fasten securely.

Right Thumb. Transfer 13 gusset stitches onto 2 needles. With SMB facing, rejoin yarns, working 1 D stitch over D stitch then resuming S&P throughout the round. Pick up 6 stitches at the base of the thumb (19 stitches). Work 11 rounds or desired length in S&P. Work Finger Decrease Rounds 1 and 2.

Left Hand. Set Up Round. Round 1. Join yarns and work SMB chart on needle 1 for the front of the mitten. Work Round 1 of S&P until 5 stitches remain in the round. Place marker. Work Round 1 of the thumb gusset chart. Place marker. The thumb gusset is now in position for the left hand. **Round 2.** Work Round 2 of SMB chart, Round 2 in S&P on the palm. Slip marker. Work Round 2 of thumb gusset chart (increase round). Slip marker.

Continue working successive rounds of SMB on the front of the mitten, S&P on the palm and thumb gusset chart, until Round 12 is complete. There are 11 D stitches between the 2 D outline stitches.

Round 13. Work Round 13 of SMB chart. Work S&P to marker. Remove marker. Slip 13 thumb gusset stitches onto a holder. Cast on 5 stitches in correct colour sequence to bridge the gap. Remove marker. The left thumb gusset is now complete (47 stitches). Beginning with Round 14, continue left hand in same manner as right until Round 21 is complete. Break yarns.

Left Index Finger. Slip 2 stitches from end of needle 3 onto the beginning of needle 1 (23 stitches on needle 1). Slip last 7 stitches from needle 3 and the first 7 stitches of needle 1 onto waste yarn for the index finger.

Left Hand. With SMB facing, rejoin yarns. Work S&P on front and palm of the mitten, casting on 4 stitches in correct colour sequence to bridge the gap. Work 8 rounds more, or desired length, in S&P. **Next Round.** Work S&P to last 2 stitches. Slip these 2 stitches to the beginning of needle 1 (front of the mitten). Arrange stitches as follows. Needle 1: 18 stitches. Needle 2: 10 stitches. Needle 3: 9 stitches. Proceed to Shape Top.

Left Index Finger. With SMB facing, slip the 7 stitches from front holder to needle 1. Slip remaining 7 stitches from the waste yarn onto another needle. With SMB facing, rejoin yarns at the right edge of the mitten, and keeping S&P correct, work the 7 stitches of needle 1. With another needle, pick up and knit 5 stitches at the base of the finger in the correct colour sequence. Work remaining 7 stitches in S&P. Complete the left index finger as the right.

Left Thumb. Transfer 13 gusset stitches onto 2 needles. With palm facing, rejoin yarns and complete in the same manner as right thumb.

Finishing. Carefully darn all ends, paying particular attention to the areas where yarns were broken and joined. Correct puckers and loose stitches as you darn. Trim darned ends neatly. Press gently under a damp cloth, omitting ribbing.

© Christine LeGrow 2018

FOGO ISLAND NINE PATCH
Classic Mittens for Ladies

DEGREE OF DIFFICULTY: ✳ ✳ TANGLY

Fogo Island (N49°40', W54°11') is a place of large personalities and landscapes, and intriguing history. It is a photographer's dream. It is home to fishermen, artists, and those seeking a simpler way of life. There is nothing simple, however, about Fogo Island itself. It is a complex place. Barren and wild as anyone who witnesses a winter gale or spring ice can confirm, yet rich in human warmth and culture. Picture caribou roaming the tundra, colourful fishing boats tied up in a storm, crisply painted houses, potato gardens in flower, and clotheslines draped with favourite quilts waving in a summer breeze. The Double Irish Chain and Nine Patch quilt patterns are the inspiration for these mittens. Colour choice alone determines the result.

Fogo means "fire" in Portuguese. The island had a migratory fishery established by the French in the 17th century, and by the 18th century permanent English and Irish settlers had arrived. Fogo Island is located off the northeast coast of the island of Newfoundland. Accessible by ferry, its residents always have a warm welcome for visitors.

MATERIALS

Briggs and Little Sport 1-ply wool. 1 skein Dark (D), 1 skein Light (L) for a two-colour mitten as shown at left. Multicoloured version requires oddments of 7 colours. 1 set each double-pointed needles size 2.50 mm and 3.00 mm, ring markers, darning needle, stitch holders.

SIZE

Ladies' Medium. Circumference: 8.5 inches (22.5 cm). Length measured from beginning of the Fogo chart to the cast off: 7.5 inches (18 cm).

GAUGE

24 stitches x 17 rows = 2 inches (5 cm) in S&P, using 3 mm needles.

SALT AND PEPPER PATTERN (S&P)

Worked over an odd number of stitches.
Round 1. (K1D, K1L). Repeat to end of round.
Round 2. (K1L, K1D). Repeat to end of round.

FOGO ISLAND NINE PATCH CHART

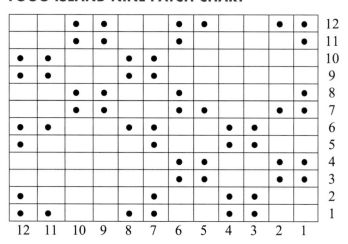

- ● K1D Empty square = K1L

Mitten front totals 30 stitches. Work stitches 1–12 twice, then stitches 1–6 once. The 2-colour mitten is 36 pattern rounds. The multicolour mitten is 42 pattern rounds.

FOGO ISLAND NINE PATCH THUMB GUSSET CHART

- ● K1D Empty square = K1L
- ⇐ Make 1 Left with L ⇒ Make 1 Right with L

The Fogo Island Nine Patch pattern is written for 2 colours. To knit multicoloured mittens, select the colours beforehand.

To carry the colour not in use more than 3 stitches, weave it through the back of the work to maintain elasticity. Instructions are for the right hand, with additional instructions for left hand and both hands where necessary. Changes required for the multicoloured Fogo Island Nine Patch mittens are included at the end of this pattern. Please read all instructions before casting on.

Work charts from right to left, bottom to top.

Always carry D on the left and L on the right to prevent streaks in the work.

Wrist. Both Hands. With D and 2.50 mm double-pointed needles, cast on 52 stitches. Join in a round, being careful not to twist. Work (K3, P1) rib for 6 rounds. Join L. Rib alternate rounds of L and D for 20 rounds. Rib 5 rounds with D. **Next Round.** With D, knit, increasing 14 stitches evenly spaced (66 stitches).

Right Hand. Set Up. Arrange stitches as follows. Needle 1 (front of mitten): 30 stitches. Needle 2: 20 stitches. Needle 3: 16 stitches. Change to 3.00 mm double-pointed needles.

Keeping D to the left and L to the right throughout, and weaving in unused colour, work Round 1 of Fogo chart on 30 stitches (front of mitten) as follows. Work stitches 1–12 twice. Work stitches 1–6 once. Place marker. K1D, K1L, K1D, K1L, K1D. Place marker. These 5 stitches form the base of the right thumb gusset and are shown as Round 1 on the Fogo Island thumb gusset chart. Work Round 1 of S&P to end of round (palm of mitten). Next round. Work Round 2 of Fogo Island chart. Slip marker. Work Round 2 (increase round) of thumb gusset chart. Slip marker. Work Round 2 of S&P to end of round.

Continue in this manner, working successive rounds of Fogo Island chart on the front, thumb gusset chart and S&P on the palm until 21 rounds are complete. **Round 22.** Work Fogo Island chart. Remove marker. Slip 19 thumb gusset stitches on a holder. Remove marker. Cast on 6 stitches in correct colour sequence to bridge the gap. Work S&P to

end of round (67 stitches). Thumb gusset is now complete and the 6 cast on stitches will form the base of the thumb.

Left Hand. Set Up. Arrange stitches on the needles as follows. Needle 1: 30 stitches (front of mitten). Needle 2: 16 stitches. Needle 3: 20 stitches. Change to 3.00 mm double-pointed needles.

Work Fogo Island chart Round 1 on first 30 stitches as follows. Work stitches 1–12 twice. Work stitches 1–6 once. Work Round 1 of S&P to last 5 stitches. Place marker. Work Round 1 thumb gusset chart. Place marker. **Next Round.** Work Fogo Island chart Round 2 on first 30 stitches. Work S&P to last 5 stitches. Slip marker. Work Round 2 (increase round) of thumb gusset chart.

Continue in this manner as established until Round 21 is complete. **Round 22.** Work Round 22 of Fogo Island chart. Work S&P to marker. Remove marker. Slip next 19 stitches on a holder. Cast on 6 stitches in correct colour sequence to bridge the gap (67 stitches). Thumb gusset is now complete.

Both Hands. Work Round 23 of Fogo Island chart on the front of the mitten. Work S&P on the palm, completing the round. Continue working the front of the mitten in Fogo Island and the palm in S&P until Round 36 of the Fogo Island chart is complete and palm is worked in S&P to end of round. Work 7 rounds S&P or until mitten reaches tip of little finger. **Right Hand. Set Up for Top Shaping.** Slip first 3 stitches from needle 2 to the end of needle 1, which holds the front of the mitten (needle 1: 33, needle 2: 17, needle 3:17).

Left Hand. Set Up for Top Shaping. Work in S&P on needles 1 and 2. Needle 3. Work in S&P until 3 stitches remain. Slip these 3 stitches to the beginning of needle 1, which holds the front of the mitten (needle 1: 33, needle 2: 17, needle 3: 17).

Both Hands. Shape Top. Decreases are made 1 stitch in from the edge at 4 points in the round. 2 decrease rounds are followed by a round with no decreases.

Shaping Round 1. Needle 1. K1 in correct colour sequence. SSK with the next colour in the sequence. Resume pattern on next stitch, having made 2 stitches of the same colour. Work in pattern until 3 stitches remain before the end of the needle. K2tog in the same colour as the stitch just made. Work last stitch in correct colour in sequence. **Needle 2.** K1, SSK as above, work in pattern to end of needle. **Needle 3.** Work in pattern until 3 stitches remain in round. K2tog in the same colour as the stitch just made. K1 in correct colour. **Shaping Round 2.** Work SSK and K2tog decreases at the same points as in the previous round. Correct colour sequence will be restored. **Shaping Round 3.** Work in S&P without decreasing.

Repeat these 3 rounds until 27 stitches remain, ending after Shaping Round 3 is complete. Break yarns, leaving a dark tail approximately 12 inches (30 cm) long for the 3-needle bind off and a short light tail sufficient for darning. Cast off using 3-needle bind off.

3-Needle Bind Off. Place the stitches from the front of the mitten on a length of waste yarn. Place the stitches of the palm on another length of waste yarn. Turn the mitten inside out to work the bind off on the wrong side. Return the stitches from the yarns onto 2 2.50 mm double-pointed needles. Hold these needles parallel to one another. Have the needle with the greater number of stitches nearest you. With a third needle, and using the long tail of D, K1 from the holding needle nearest you. Then knit 1 stitch from the front needle together with 1 stitch of the opposite colour from the back needle. You now have 2 stitches on the working needle. Pass first stitch on the working needle over the second stitch to cast it off. 1 stitch remains on the working needle. Continue to knit together 1 stitch from the front and back needles and slipping the first stitch over the second stitch on the working needle to cast off. Repeat until

1 stitch remains. Break yarns. Thread through remaining stitch. Draw up and fasten securely.

Thumb. Both Hands. Place the 19 gusset stitches on 2 needles. Rejoin yarn. K1D over the D stitch, then resume S&P to last stitch. K1D. Using a third needle, and keeping S&P correct, pick up and knit 6 stitches at the base of the thumb (25 stitches). Continue to knit rounds of S&P until thumb measures 2.25 inches (6 cm), or desired length.

Thumb Decrease Round 1. (Knit first stitch in correct colour sequence. K2tog with next colour. K1 with same colour as the stitch just worked). Repeat to end of round, knitting any remaining stitches in S&P. **Thumb Decrease Round 2.** (K1, K2tog) in S&P to end of round, working any remaining stitches in S&P. Break yarns. Thread through remaining stitches. Draw up and fasten securely.

Finishing. Carefully darn in all ends and trim neatly. Press carefully under a damp cloth, omitting ribbing.

FOGO ISLAND NINE PATCH MULTICOLOUR MITTEN

For the 7-colour version, make the following changes as you work. Choose 3 L shades and 3 D shades, plus 1 shade in between that complements the others. With the complementary shade, cast on in the same manner as the instructions for the 2-colour mitten. Throughout the ribbed cuff, add 6 additional colours in any order. Proceed using colours in the following sequence.

Rounds 1–6. A-Dark and B-Light. Break A and B.
Rounds 7–12. C-Dark and D-Light. Break C and D.
Rounds 13–18. E-Dark and F-Light. Break E and F.

Repeat these 18 rounds once more. Join A-Dark and B-Light. Work Rounds 1–6. 42 rounds of the Fogo Island chart are complete. Break A and B. Rejoin the colours of your choice to work the top, incorporating the complementary shade as 1 of the 2 colours. Work 1 round of S&P before following the Right and Left Top Shaping instructions.

Work Thumbs in A-Dark and B-Light.

© Christine LeGrow 2018

WEE ONES
Thumbless Mitts for Babies

DEGREE OF DIFFICULTY: ✳ EASY DOES IT

Parents lovingly collect baby's first treasures, first picture book, first teddy bear, and first shoes. Here is a choice of first mittens for your very own Little Nipper or Treasure Trout.

Our Wee Ones are thumbless. No need for gussets. They fit the tiniest member of the family. Choose the quick and easy chart of your choice and a couple of contrasting colours of leftover yarn—about the size of an orange for each will complete a pair. Load up the needles and have fun knitting these to keep tiny hands warm.

SIZE

To fit 3 months to 1 year. Circumference: 6 inches (15 cm). Length of hand from the first round of Wee Ones chart to the tip of the cast off: 3.25 inches (8 cm).

MATERIALS

Briggs and Little Regal 2-ply worsted weight yarn, oddments of Dark (D) and Light (L). 1 set 3.25 mm double-pointed needles. Two thinner double-pointed needles for bind off only.

Ring markers, darning needle, two 6-inch (15 cm) lengths of contrasting colour yarn.

GAUGE

12 stitches x 14 rounds = 2 inches (5 cm) worked over S&P, using 3.25 mm needles.

WEE ONES DIAMONDS CHART

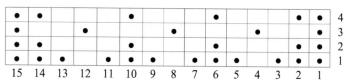

Work Rounds 1 to 4 four times, then Round 1 once (17 rounds).

WEE ONES SQUARES CHART

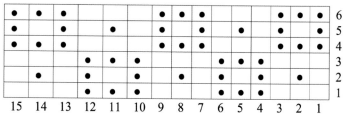

Work Rounds 1 to 6 twice, then Rounds 1 to 3 once (15 rounds).

WEE ONES TRIANGLES CHART

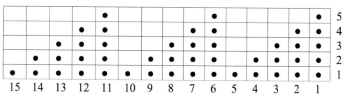

Work Rounds 1 to 5 three times (15 rounds).

•   K1D   Empty square = K1L

SALT AND PEPPER PATTERN (S&P)

Worked over an odd number of stitches.

Round 1. (K1D, K1L). Repeat to end of round.

Round 2. (K1L, K1D). Repeat to end of round.

Left and right mittens are identical. Before beginning, determine whether wrists will be solid or striped. Choose which pair to knit: Diamonds, Squares, or Triangles. Each has an easy chart. The Diamonds chart is 2 rounds longer than the Squares or Triangles. The charts are referred to as WO in the pattern.

Work charts from right to left, bottom to top. Always carry D to the left and L to the right to avoid streaks in the colour work. Please read all instructions before casting on.

Wrist. With 3.25 mm needles and D, cast on 28 stitches. Join in a round, being careful not to twist. Work (K1, P1) rib for 14 rounds, increasing 3 stitches evenly spaced on final round (31 stitches). When carrying the colour not in use more than 3 stitches, weave it in every 3 stitches to maintain elasticity.

Arrange stitches as follows. Needle 1: 15 stitches (front of mitten). Needles 2 and 3 share 16 palm stitches.

Round 1. Front. Join L. Work Round 1 of WO chart of your choice from right to left. **Palm.** Work Round 1 of S&P on palm of the mitten. **Round 2.** Work Round 2 of WO chart on front of the mitten. Work Round 2 of S&P on palm. Continue in established manner until the final round of WO is complete. **Next Round.** Work 15 D stitches on the front of the mitten. Work S&P to end of round. Work 1 round in S&P.

Shape Top. On odd numbered rounds, decreasing will create 2 adjacent stitches in the same colour. On the following even numbered rounds, these stitches will be worked together, restoring the correct colour sequence.

Decreases are made 1 stitch in from the edge of front and palm at 4 points in the round.

Shaping Round 1. Needle 1. K1 in correct colour. SSK with the next colour in the sequence. Resume pattern on the next

The three little kittens
They lost their mittens
And they began to cry.
O mother dear we greatly fear
our mittens we have lost.
What, lost your mittens?
You naughty kittens!
Then you shall have no pie.

—TRADITIONAL NURSERY RHYME

stitch (having made 2 adjacent stitches in the same colour). Work in pattern until 3 stitches remain before the end of the needle. K2tog in the same colour as the stitch just made. Work last stitch in the correct colour. **Needle 2.** K1, SSK as above. Work in pattern to the end of the needle. **Needle 3.** Work in pattern until 3 stitches remain before the end of the round. K2tog in the same colour as the stitch just made. K1 in correct colour. **Shaping Round 2.** Work SSK and K2tog at the same points as the previous round. Correct colour sequence will be restored. Repeat these 2 shaping rounds until 15 stitches remain. Cast off using 3-needle bind off.

3-Needle Bind Off. Place the stitches from the front of the mitten on a length of waste yarn. Place the stitches of the palm on another length of waste yarn. Turn the mitten inside out to work the bind off on the wrong side. Return the stitches from the yarns onto 2 thinner double-pointed needles. Hold these needles parallel to one another. Have the needle with the greater number of stitches facing you. With a third needle, and using the long tail of D, K1 from the holding needle nearest you. Then knit 1 stitch from the front needle together with 1 stitch of the opposite colour from the back needle. You now have 2 stitches on the working needle. Pass first stitch on the working needle over the second stitch to cast it off. 1 stitch remains on the working needle. Continue to knit together 1 stitch from the front and back needles and slipping the first stitch over the second stitch on the working needle to cast off. Repeat until 1 stitch remains. Fasten off and darn in ends.

Make an identical mitten.

Finishing. Carefully darn in ends. Trim neatly. Press under a damp cloth, omitting ribbing.

© Christine LeGrow 2018

NOR'EASTER
Gloves or Classic Mittens for Ladies

DEGREE OF DIFFICULTY: ✳ ✳ ✳ OVER THE WHARF

A rush of towering waves, a swirl of stinging snow, the fierce snarl of an icy wind and another nor'easter is upon us. After brooding for days and gaining strength over countless miles of ocean, it hurls itself onto our shores. In a place where spectacular weather events are commonplace, nor'easters are among our most dramatic storms.

Wave patterns appear frequently in traditional Newfoundland mittens. This unusual one was a happy accident, created when incorrectly charting the stitch pattern of a vintage mitten.

SIZE

Ladies' Medium. Circumference: 8 inches (20.5 cm). Length: 11 inches (28 cm) from cast on to tip of middle finger. Thumb: 2.25 inches (6 cm). Index finger: 2.75 inches (7 cm). Middle finger: 3 inches (8 cm). Ring finger: 2.75 inches (7 cm). Baby finger: 2.25 inches (6 cm). Length of thumb and fingers is adjustable.

MATERIALS

1 set of 4.00 mm double-pointed needles. 1 skein Briggs and Little Regal 2-ply worsted weight wool in Dark (D). 1 skein Briggs and Little Regal 2-ply worsted weight wool in Light (L). Ring markers, lengths of waste yarn for stitch holders.

GAUGE

24 stitches x 28 rows = 4 inches (10 cm).

SALT AND PEPPER PATTERN (S&P)

Worked over an odd number of stitches.
Round 1. (K1D, K1L). Repeat to end of round.
Round 2. (K1L, K1D). Repeat to end of round.

NOR'EASTER RIGHT HAND (6 stitches x 6 rows)

NOR'EASTER THUMB GUSSET CHART

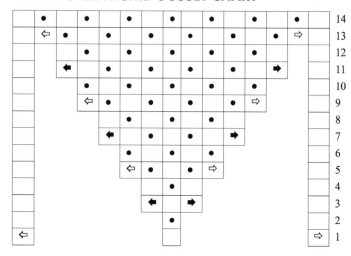

NOR'EASTER LEFT HAND (6 stitches x 6 rows)

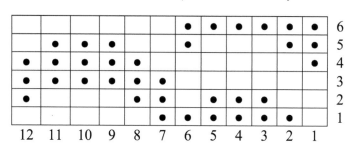

● K1D Empty square = K1L

→ Make 1 Right with D ← Make 1 Left with D

⇦ Make 1 Left with L ⇨ Make 1 Right with L

Work charts from right to left, bottom to top. Always carry D on the left and L on the right to prevent streaks in the work. Instructions apply to both hands unless otherwise stated.

Wrist. With D, cast on 36 stitches. Divide evenly on 3 needles and join in a circle, being careful not to twist. Work 27 rounds of (K2, P1) rib in a striped pattern of your choice. **Next Round.** With D, knit, increasing 13 stitches (49 stitches). Arrange work 24, 13, 12 stitches.

Round 1. Right Hand. Front. Join L and keeping D ahead (i.e., on the left) throughout, work Round 1 of Nor'easter Right Hand chart 2 times. These 24 stitches form the front of the mitten. **Palm.** K1L, K1D. Place marker. Work Round 1 of thumb gusset chart. Place marker. (K1D, K1L) to end of round. These stitches form the palm. **Left Hand. Front.** Join L and, keeping D ahead (i.e., on the left) throughout, work Round 1 of Nor'easter Left Hand chart twice. These 24 stitches form the front of the mitten. **Palm.** (K1L, K1D) until 3 stitches remain in round. Place marker. Work Round 1 of thumb gusset chart. Place marker. K1D, K1L.

Both Hands. This sets up the Nor'easter pattern on the front and S&P on the palm and places the point of the thumb gusset with its two L outline stitches between the markers.

Round 2. Front. Work Round 2 of Nor'easter chart for the correct hand. **Palm.** Work in S&P to marker. Slip marker. Work Round 2 of thumb gusset chart to marker. Slip marker. Work in S&P to end of round. Note that beginning with gusset

Photo: J. Loaning

Round 3, gusset increases are made within the outline stitches on every second round, in the colour indicated.

Continue working successive rounds of Nor'easter on the front of the mitten, S&P on the palm, and the thumb gusset within the markers until gusset Round 14 is complete, finishing the row in S&P (15 gusset stitches between markers). **Next Round.** Work in patterns as established to marker. Remove marker. Place 15 gusset stitches on a holder. Remove marker. Make 1 with correct S&P colour to bridge the gap. Work in pattern to end of round (49 stitches).

Continue working Nor'easter on the front and S&P on the palm until 24 rounds of Nor'easter are complete. Finish the palm in S&P.

MITTEN ONLY

Beginning with K1L, work 1 round of S&P on all stitches (49 stitches). Continue for 12 rounds more in S&P, or until work reaches the tip of the little finger, ending with Nor'easter facing for next round.

Shape Picket-Fence Top. Decreases are made 1 stitch in from the edge at 4 points in the round, positioned as on the toe of a sock. Decreases are made on every round.

Shaping Round 1. Front. K1 in correct colour. SSK with the next colour in the sequence. Resume S&P pattern on next stitch, having made 2 adjacent stitches of the same colour. Work in pattern until 3 stitches remain on front. K2tog in the same colour as the stitch just made. Work last stitch in correct colour. **Palm.** As front.

Shaping Round 2. Front. K1. SSK in next colour. Work S&P until 3 stitches remain on front. K2tog in same colour as the stitch just made. K1. **Palm.** As front. Correct colour sequence is restored.

Repeat these 2 shaping rounds until there are too few stitches left to continue decreasing (9 stitches remain). Break yarns. Thread D into a darning needle and pass through remaining stitches. Tighten and secure. Proceed to Thumb.

GLOVE ONLY

Cut 6 lengths of waste yarn to hold finger stitches.

Right Hand. Front. Break yarns. With Nor'easter facing and beginning at the right edge of the glove, put 6 stitches on holder for baby finger. Put next 6 stitches on holder for ring finger. Put next 6 stitches on holder for middle finger. **Palm.** Put corresponding 6 stitches on holder for baby finger, 6 stitches for ring finger, 6 stitches for middle finger. 13 stitches remain for index finger.

Left Hand. Front. With Nor'easter facing and beginning at the left edge of the glove, place 6 stitches on holder for baby finger. Put next 6 stitches on holder for ring finger. Place next 6 stitches on holder for middle finger. **Palm.** Place corresponding 6 stitches of palm on holder for baby finger. 6 stitches for ring finger. 6 stitches for middle finger. 13 stitches remain for index finger.

Right Index Finger. With Nor'easter facing, rejoin yarns. Beginning with K1L, work 13 stitches in S&P. Cast on 6 stitches in correct S&P sequence (19 stitches). Divide work on 3 needles and join in a circle. Note beginning of round. Work 15 rounds more of S&P, or until work reaches the tip of the finger. Work Finger Decrease Rounds 1 and 2.

Right Middle Finger. Transfer 6 stitches from front and 6 from palm to double-pointed needles. With Nor'easter facing, rejoin yarns and beginning with K1L work stitches in S&P. Pick up and knit 5 stitches in correct colour order from the base of the index finger. Work palm stitches in S&P. Cast on 2 stitches in correct S&P order (19 stitches). Divide work on 3 needles and join in a circle. Note beginning of round. Work 17 rounds more in S&P, or until work reaches the tip of the finger. Work Finger Decrease Rounds 1 and 2.

Right Ring Finger. Transfer 6 stitches from front and 6 from palm to double-pointed needles. With Nor'easter facing, rejoin yarns and beginning with K1L, work stitches

in S&P. Pick up and knit 3 stitches in correct colour order from the base of the middle finger. Work palm stitches in S&P. Cast on 4 stitches in correct S&P order (19 stitches). Divide work on 3 needles and join in a circle. Note beginning of round. Work 15 rounds more in S&P, or until work reaches the tip of the finger. Work Finger Decrease Rounds 1 and 2.

Right Baby Finger. Transfer 6 stitches from front and 6 from palm to double-pointed needles. With Nor'easter facing, rejoin yarns and, beginning with K1L, work stitches in S&P. Pick up and knit 5 stitches in correct colour order from the base of the ring finger. Work palm stitches in S&P (17 stitches). Divide work on 3 needles and join in a circle. Note beginning of round. Work 12 rounds more in S&P, or until work reaches the tip of the finger. Work Finger Decrease Rounds 1 and 2.

Left Index Finger. With Nor'easter facing, and beginning with K1L, work 6 front stitches in S&P. Cast on 6 stitches in correct S&P order. Work 7 palm stitches in S&P (19 stitches). Divide work on 3 needles, join in a circle and note beginning of round. Work 15 rounds more of S&P, or until work reaches the tip of the finger. Work Finger Decrease Rounds 1 and 2.

Left Middle Finger. Transfer 6 stitches from front and 6 from palm to double-pointed needles. With Nor'easter facing, rejoin yarns and beginning with K1L work front stitches in

S&P. Cast on 4 stitches in correct S&P order. Work 6 palm stitches in S&P. Pick up and knit 3 stitches in correct colour order from the base of the index finger (19 stitches). Divide work on 3 needles and join in a circle. Note beginning of round. Work 17 rounds more in S&P, or until work reaches the tip of the finger. Work Finger Decrease Rounds 1 and 2.

Left Ring Finger. Transfer 6 stitches from front and 6 from palm to double-pointed needles. With Nor'easter facing, rejoin yarns and, beginning with K1L, work front stitches in S&P. Cast on 4 stitches in correct S&P order. Work palm stitches in S&P. Pick up and knit 3 stitches in correct colour order from the base of the middle finger (19 stitches). Divide work on 3 needles and join in a circle. Note beginning of round. Work 15 rounds more in S&P, or until work reaches the tip of the finger. Work Finger Decrease Rounds 1 and 2.

Left Baby Finger. Transfer 6 stitches from front and 6 from palm to double-pointed needles. With Nor'easter facing, rejoin yarns and beginning with K1L, work front stitches in S&P. Work palm stitches in S&P. Pick up and knit 5 stitches in correct colour order from the base of the ring finger (17 stitches). Divide work on 3 needles and join in a circle. Note beginning of round. Work 12 rounds more in S&P, or until work reaches the tip of the finger. Work Finger Decrease Rounds 1 and 2.

Nor'easter Classic Mitten.

Photo: J. Loenning

Photo: J. Loaning

Finger Decrease Round 1. (K1 with correct colour in S&P sequence. K2tog with next colour in sequence. K1 in S&P). Repeat to end of round, working any leftover stitches in S&P. Adjacent stitches in the same colour will be eliminated in the next round. **Finger Decrease Round 2.** (K1 with correct S&P colour. K2tog with next colour in S&P sequence). Repeat to end of round, working any leftover stitches in S&P. Break yarns. Thread through remaining stitches and secure.

Thumb. Transfer thumb stitches from holder to 2 double-pointed needles. Rejoin yarns and knit these stitches in S&P. With another needle, pick up and knit 4 stitches in S&P at the base of the thumb (19 stitches). Work 12 rounds more in S&P. Work Finger Decrease Rounds 1 and 2.

Finishing. Darn ends securely. Press well, omitting ribbing.

BLOWIN' A GALE
Trigger Mitts for Men

DEGREE OF DIFFICULTY: ✳✳ TANGLY

More often than not it is blowin' a gale on the island of Newfoundland. The capital city of St. John's is ranked third windiest city in the world. It is almost never "flat cam" (translation: no wind). When a gale warning is issued to mariners, ships seek port, fisherfolk stay ashore, and the laundry does not go on the line! These trigger mitts remind us of choppy seas spattered with ice or topped with whitecaps and the sting of the sea spray on your cheeks.

SIZE

Men's Large. Circumference: 10.25 inches (26 cm). Length measured from beginning of pattern to tip cast off: 9.25 inches (23.5 cm).

MATERIALS

Briggs and Little Heritage worsted weight wool, 1 skein Dark (D), 1 skein Light (L). 1 set of double-pointed needles size 3.25 mm. Ring markers, darning needle, stitch holders.

GAUGE

18 stitches x 18 rounds = 3 inches (7.5 cm) in S&P pattern, using 3.25 mm needles.

SALT AND PEPPER PATTERN (S&P)

Worked on an odd number of stitches.

Round 1. (K1D, K1L). Repeat to end of round.
Round 2. (K1L, K1D). Repeat to end of round.

BLOWIN' A GALE RIGHT HAND

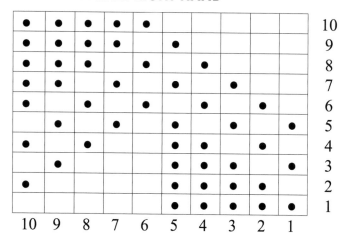

BLOWIN' A GALE LEFT HAND

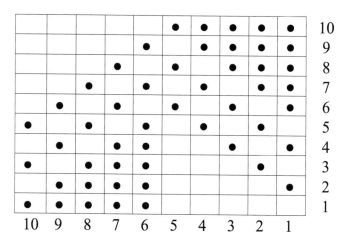

- ● K1D

Empty square = K1L

Horizontal repeat: 3 times = 30 stitches.

BLOWIN' A GALE THUMB GUSSET CHART

- ● K1D
- ⇐ Make 1 Left with L

Empty square = K1L

⇒ Make 1 Right with L

Work charts from right to left, bottom to top. Always carry D on the left and L on the right to prevent streaks in the work. Instructions are for both hands except where indicated. Please read all instructions carefully before casting on.

Wrist. Using D, cast on 48 stitches. Join in a round, being careful not to twist. Work 3 rounds (K2, P1) ribbing. Join L and work alternate rounds of L and D ribbing for 17 rounds, ending with a L round. With D, work 4 rounds ribbing, increasing 11 stitches evenly spaced on last round (59 stitches).

Right Hand. Arrange stitches as follows. Needle 1: 30 stitches (front of mitten). Needle 2: 17 stitches. Needle 3: 12 stitches. **Round 1.** Work Round 1 of the Right Hand Blowin' a Gale (RHBG) chart 3 times on 30 front stitches. Place marker. Work Round 1 of thumb gusset chart. Place marker. Work Round 1 of S&P to the end of the round. **Round 2.** Work Round 2 of RHBG chart. Slip marker. Work Round 2 (increase round) of the thumb gusset chart. Slip marker. Work Round 2 of S&P to the end of the round for the palm of the mitten. Continue working successive rounds of RHBG chart, thumb gusset, and S&P on the palm as established until Round 21 is complete. **Round 22.** Work Round 22 of RHBG chart. Remove marker. K1D over the D outline stitch. Slip the 17 thumb gusset stitches on a holder. Cast on 5 stitches in the correct colour sequence to bridge the gap. K1 in S&P. Remove marker. Work S&P on palm. Thumb gusset is now complete (61 stitches). Continue until Round 29 is complete.

Right Index Finger Set Up. Work final round of RHBG chart on 30 stitches of needle 1. Slip the last 9 stitches just worked to a needle for the front of the index finger. Slip the first 9 stitches of needle 2 to another needle and work these 9 stitches in S&P for the back of the index finger. Slip all remaining palm and front stitches onto holders.

Right Index Finger. Cast on 5 stitches in correct colour

Wind and Fog are a mariner's natural enemies. Winds can reach a velocity of 140 km/hour at St. John's Airport, with gusts up to 200 km/hour. Winds on Signal Hill, and on open waters, are generally more severe.

Le vent et la brume sont les deux ennemis naturels du navigateur. À l'aéroport de Saint-Jean, le vent peut atteindre 140 km/h, avec des bourrasques atteignant les 200 km/h. Sur Signal Hill et en haute mer, les vents sont généralement plus intenses.

sequence (23 stitches). Divide evenly on 3 needles and work in S&P for 17 rounds or desired length.

Finger Decrease Round 1. (K1 with correct S&P colour. K2tog with next colour in sequence. K1 in S&P). Repeat to end of round, knitting any leftover stitches in S&P. **Finger Decrease Round 2.** (K1, K2tog) in S&P to end of round, working any remaining stitches in S&P. Break yarns. Thread through remaining stitches. Draw up and fasten securely.

Right Hand. Slip the stitches from the holder and arrange as follows. Needle 1: 21 stitches. Needles 2 and 3 share the remaining stitches. With palm facing, rejoin yarns and work in correct S&P sequence to the index finger. Pick up and knit 4 stitches at the base of the finger in correct colour sequence and complete the round (47 stitches). Work S&P for 12 rounds more, or until work reaches the tip of the little finger.

Right Hand Top Shaping Set Up. Slip 2 stitches from the end of needle 1 (front of mitten) onto the beginning of needle

2. Arrange stitches as follows. Needle 1: 23 stitches. Needle 2: 12 stitches. Needle 3: 12 stitches. Proceed to Shape Top.

Left Hand. Arrange stitches as follows. Needle 1: 30 stitches (front of mitten). Needle 2: 12 stitches (beginning of palm). Needle 3: 17 stitches (remainder of palm, and base of thumb gusset). **Round 1.** Work Round 1 of Left Hand Blowin' a Gale (LHBG) chart (front of mitten). Work Round 1 of S&P on next 24 stitches for palm. Place marker. Work Round 1 of thumb gusset chart. Place marker. This establishes the front, palm, and thumb gusset for the left mitten. Work until Round 21 is complete. **Round 22.** Work Round 22 of LHBG chart. Work S&P to marker. Remove marker. K1L over the D outline stitch. Slip 17 gusset stitches onto a holder. Cast on 5 stitches in the correct colour sequence to bridge the gap. K1L over the remaining D outline stitch. Remove marker. Left thumb gusset is now complete. Continue as for right hand until Round 29 is complete.

Left Index Finger. Work Round 30 of LHBG chart on needle 1. Break yarns. Slip the first 9 stitches of needle 1 to another needle. Slip the remaining stitches of needle 1 (front of mitten) and all but the last 9 stitches of the palm to a holder. With palm facing, rejoin yarns and keeping S&P correct, knit the 9 stitches remaining on needle 3 and the 9 stitches on needle 1. With another needle, cast on 5 stitches in correct colour sequence (23 stitches). Complete as right index finger.

Left Hand. With palm facing, rejoin yarns. Pick up and knit 4 stitches in the correct colour sequence at the base of the index finger. Complete the round in S&P. Work 11 rounds more of S&P.

Left Hand Top Shaping Set Up. Round 12. Work in S&P until 2 stitches remain. Slip these 2 stitches to the end of the first needle. Needle 1: 23 stitches. Needle 2:12 stitches. Needle 3: 12 stitches. Proceed to Shape Top.

Shape Top. On odd numbered rounds, decreasing will create two adjacent stitches of the same colour. On the following even numbered decrease rounds, these stitches will be worked

together, restoring the correct colour sequence. Decreases are made 1 stitch in from the edge at 4 points in the round.

Shaping Round 1. Needle 1. K1 in correct colour. SSK with the next colour in the sequence. Resume pattern on the next stitch (having made 2 adjacent stitches of same colour). Work S&P until 3 stitches remain before the end of the needle. K2tog in the same colour as the stitch just made. Work the last stitch in correct colour. **Needle 2.** K1, SSK with next colour in the sequence. Work in pattern to the end of the needle. **Needle 3.** Work in pattern until 3 stitches remain before the end of the needle. K2tog in the same colour as the stitch just made. K1 in correct colour. **Shaping Round 2.** Work SSK and K2tog decreases in S&P at the same points as the previous round. Correct colour sequence will be restored. Repeat these 2 shaping rounds until 15 stitches remain. Break yarns, leaving a D tail approximately 12 inches (30 cm) long to complete the bind off and a short L tail sufficient for darning. Cast off, using 3-needle bind off.

3-Needle Bind Off. Place stitches from the front of the mitten on a length of waste yarn. Place the stitches of the palm on another length of waste yarn. Turn the mitten inside out to work the bind off on the wrong side. Return the stitches from the holders to 2 thinner double-pointed needles for convenience. Hold these needles parallel to one another. Have the needle with the greater number of stitches nearest you. With a third needle and using the long tail of D, knit 1 stitch from the holding needle nearest you. Then knit 1 stitch from the front needle together with 1 stitch of the opposite colour from the back needle. You now have 2 stitches on the working needle. Pass first stitch on the working needle over the second stitch to cast it off. 1 stitch remains on the working needle. Continue to knit together 1 stitch from the front and back needles and slipping the first stitch over the second stitch on the working needle to cast off. Repeat until 1 stitch remains. Thread through remaining stitch. Draw up and fasten securely.

Thumb. Slip 17 thumb gusset stitches onto 2 needles. With

Hand carder:
Flat implement with wire teeth, used in pairs to comb wool for spinning; card. "We had the old-time carders, the two hand-carders. But now they got the carders what you turned around, revolved."
—DICTIONARY OF NEWFOUNDLAND ENGLISH

needle 3, pick up and knit in the correct colour sequence 8 stitches at the base of the thumb. Work these 25 thumb stitches for 15 rounds, or desired length. Work Finger Decrease Rounds 1 and 2.

Finishing. Carefully darn all ends and trim neatly. Press carefully under a damp cloth, omitting ribbing.

© Christine LeGrow 2018

ACKNOWLEDGEMENTS

We would like to thank all of those who have encouraged us in this work. We have received a particular helping hand from the following people and organizations:

Robin Hansen and Janetta Dexter, whose pioneering work on North Atlantic mittens 40 years ago was a catalyst.

Dr. Phil Hiscock and Jasmine Paul, folklorists, for putting us in touch with the knitters of old.

Mary Dawn Greenwood, whose inspired sense of colour pioneered some of the nicest combinations in this collection.

Milly Brown, Suzanne Molloy, and Denise Moss, our dedicated test knitters, patiently reknit everything and uncovered our bloopers. Thank goodness.

Mary Nippard and others, who helped spark the connection between diamonds in mittens and architecture.

The geology of Newfoundland is spectacular. Some of our photos were taken on the famous rocks displayed in front of the Johnson Geo Centre on Signal Hill. Our thanks to them for showcasing the wonders of our province so beautifully.

Becky Williams, whose lively encouragement provided us with an ambitious deadline that we stuck to, even when one of us would have preferred to stroll more leisurely along the path to authorship.

Staff and management of Posie Row & Co., for granting permission to use the fine old interior of their shop as a location.

St. Thomas' Anglican Church, for permission to take photographs on their heritage premises.

Artist Barbara Daniell, for assistance with information and photographs about the *Finding Beauty* installation in Gros Morne National Park.

Artist Peter Sobol, for permission to use his quotation and his charming image *Some Toasty*.

Artist and ceramic fundamentalist Michael Flaherty, for permission to relate his amazing mitten story and accompanying images.

Anne Manuel, for her help and guidance over many years and for graciously writing the foreword to this book. She has been a true mentor to us and to many others.

Photographic artist Paddy Barry, for his inspirational photos of Fogo Island.

Brian Carey, of Brian Carey Photography, for permission to reproduce the Mummers photo.

Photographer Eric Abbott, for the outstanding winter scene of the Bonavista lighthouse.

Shawn Fitzpatrick, bird photographer extraordinaire, for the photo of gannets at Cape St. Mary's.

Ross Abbott, collector of vintage photos, for permission to use two from his esteemed collection.

Jeanette Laaning, our devoted photographer, for her dedication and skill, accomplishing extraordinary yoga poses and feats of rock climbing to get the perfect shot.

Geri Ottenheimer, our hands model, for knowing how to show off a trigger mitt like a Tiffany diamond.

Book writing is easier when one has a talented and supportive family. We would like to thank Laurie LeGrow, for technical support and photography; Derrick L. LeGrow, for hand model and photographic assistance, and for THE BINDER; Derrick C. LeGrow, for hand model, technical assistance, and never-ending patience; Serena LeGrow, for her photographs; Max McMillan for assisting at the cover photo shoots; and Katherine Scott, for the inspiring mitten mandala concept.

BIBLIOGRAPHY

Baikie, Margaret. *Labrador Memories: Reflections at Mulligan*. Happy Valley-Goose Bay: Them Days Pub., 1976.

England, George Allan. *Vikings of the Ice*. Garden City, NY: Doubleday, Page & Company, 1924.

Gough, William. *The Art of David Blackwood*. Toronto: McGraw-Hill Ryerson, 1988.

Green, H. Gordon. *Don't Have Your Baby in the Dory! A Biography of Myra Bennett*. Montreal: Harvest House, 1973.

Guy, Ray. "Mysteries of the Wider World." *Atlantic Insight* (June 1989).

Hansen, Robin. *Fox & Geese & Fences: A Collection of Traditional Maine Mittens*. Camden, ME: Down East Books, 1983.

Hansen, Robin. *Favourite Mittens*. Camden, ME: Down East Books, 2005.

Hansen, Robin. *Ultimate Mittens: 28 Classic Patterns to Keep You Warm*. Camden, ME: Down East Books, 2011.

Hansen, Robin, with Janetta Dexter. *Flying Geese and Partridge Feet*. Camden, ME: Down East Books, 1986.

Hickey, Gloria. *Picking Up Lost Stitches: Research into the History of Knitting in Newfoundland*. [St. John's, NL]: Craft Council of Newfoundland and Labrador, 1999.

Knitting with Homespun. Craft Training Section, Division of Adult and Continuing Education, Department of Education, Government of Newfoundland and Labrador, 1980.

Murray, Hilda Chaulk. *More Than 50%: Woman's Life in a Newfoundland Outport 1900–1950*. St. John's: Breakwater Books, 1979.

Pocius, Gerald L. *Textile Traditions of Eastern Newfoundland*. Ottawa: National Museums of Canada, 1979.

Warner, Elizabeth S. *Knitting a Glove: One Aspect of One Woman's Knitting*, MUNFLA, 77-110.

ABOUT THE AUTHORS

CHRISTINE TEMPLEMAN LEGROW has been a knitter since early childhood. Her keen interest in preserving the traditional handknits of Newfoundland and designing new ones with the same flavour has taken her through life. Christine has been recognized by the Craft Council of Newfoundland and Labrador for these efforts and awarded both the Award of Excellence for the Preservation of Traditional Craft Skills and the Award for the Interpretation of Provincial History. Christine is the owner of Spindrift Handknits and makes her home in St. John's.

SHIRLEY A. SCOTT, sometimes known as Shirl the Purl, has been writing about knitting, designing knitwear, and publishing patterns for many years. She is the author of *Canada Knits: Craft and Comfort in a Northern Land.* She is passionate about teasing out the connections between history and craft. A Newfoundlander by choice, her creative life has flourished in her adopted home. She lives to knit in St. John's.

Christine and Shirley have collaborated on three collections of mitten patterns published by Spindrift Handknits, *Some Warm Mittens, Smiling Land Mittens,* and *'Round da Bay Mittens. Saltwater Mittens from the Island of Newfoundland* expands on their shared love of the iconic Newfoundland mitten.

Unless otherwise noted, all photos in this book were taken by Christine LeGrow.

You can contact Christine and Shirley by email with questions or just to say hello at christinelegrow@nl.rogers.com and shirlthepurl@hotmail.com.

SALTWATER MITTENS

Blowin' a Gale.

Nor'easter.

Saltwater mittens are worn by people on the sea, by the sea, or who love the sea and its traditions. The ocean in its many moods has been our muse throughout our creative lives and in the writing of this book. We love and respect the ocean. It rules our climate and our style of living.

What better way to salute the traditional mittens of Newfoundland than by acknowledging that our extreme weather dictates the need for thick, warm mittens. Patterns such as Nor'easter and Blowin' a Gale depict in knitted stitches the hungry power we see before us every day. These two patterns in particular highlight our wild weather events. When a Nor'easter is approaching it is always Blowin' a Gale. This in turn produces a storm surge which is clearly shown in the rising waves of Nor'easter.

We hope that all of our mittens, made and worn by Newfoundlanders for generations, will bring a blessing to you today.

There, a stone's throw away, was the house of Aunt Meg Feltham. It was always painted ruby red with white trim, and it had curious diamond shaped windows. One window let light into the pantry, another allowed sunshine through the upstairs hallway. Uncle Elias Feltham would look out the diamond and, on a clear day, see the way the sun itself was shattered into diamonds by the ocean.

—WILLIAM GOUGH, *THE ART OF DAVID BLACKWOOD*